Popular Marine Fish for your aquarium

Martyn Haywood

TAB BOOKS Inc.

BLUE RIDGE SUMMIT, PA. 17214

FIRST PRINTING

FIRST EDITION

First published in the U.S.A. in 1984 by TAB BOOKS Inc.

Printed in Hong Kong

Reproduction or publication of the content in any manner, without express permission of the publisher, is prohibited. No liability is assumed with respect to the use of the information herein.

Library of Congress Cataloging in Publication Data

Haywood, Martyn.
    Popular marine fish for your aquarium.

    Includes index.
    1. Marine aquarium fishes—Identification. 2. Marine
aquariums. I. Title.
SF471.1.H39   1984   639.3′42   83-4947
ISBN 0-8306-0621-1 (pbk.)

Contents

7076023

Introduction	4
Choosing and siting the aquarium	5
The water	7
Water chemistry	8
Filtration and aeration	10
Heating and lighting	13
Other equipment	15
Setting-up the aquarium	17
Decor	19
Buying your fish	21
Feeding	23
Diseases	24
Invertebrates	27
Plants	31
Aquarium selections	32
Introduction to the fish families	34
Identification guide	39
Index	110

Introduction

It is intended that this book should be used primarily as an identification guide to enable the aquarist to decide which species are best suited to him, and to provide a guide to many of the species which are usually available from aquatic hobby stores. The brief introduction to keeping marine fish and invertebrates will serve to whet the appetite of the aspiring marine hobbyist, and also provides all the essential information which is required to make a success of the beginner's first tank, and his subsequent choices of fish.

There is no doubt that the successful maintenance of marine creatures in small aquaria is considerably dependent upon the skills and patience of the aquarist, although advances made in recent years have greatly reduced the difficulty of reproducing and maintaining a simulated natural environment within the confines of a comparatively small aquarium. Anyone who has successfully kept freshwater tropical fish may feel confident of taking the step towards keeping marine fish, although there is no reason why you should not begin the hobby without having kept any other sort of fish. There are positive steps that can be taken to ensure a good chance of success and, once a balanced environment has been achieved, the beauty and magnificent colours of tropical marine fish are ample reward for the effort involved. Because marine tropical fish keeping is a relatively new branch of the fish keeping hobby there are still a great many discoveries to be made. There is the opportunity for the aquarist to investigate many new areas such as breeding techniques, in which significant advances are only recently being made.

Marine aquaria can also contain interesting invertebrates.

Choosing and siting the aquarium

Over the years aquarists have experimented with aquaria made from such diverse materials as wood and concrete, and in the early days of the hobby many laborious hours were spent trying to seal the frames of the common angle-iron tanks against the corrosive properties of sea-water. Nowadays, however, thanks to the advent of silicone rubber glass adhesive, none but the most ambitious hobbyist need look any further than at the huge range of all-glass aquaria. The prime requisite of a suitable marine aquarium is that it should involve no corrodible materials, such as metals, which may result in poisoning the tank. A number of plastic moulded tanks are available but, while chemically suitable, these are usually much too small for marine fish, in addition to which they are easily scratched.

All-glass tanks, which essentially are just five pieces of glass glued together with silicone rubber are chemically inert, extremely durable and are available in large sizes. Many manufacturers produce tanks up to 2.4m (8ft) long as standard items, with bigger ones made to order. (However, smaller tanks are quite adequate for most aquarists.) All-glass tanks have the additional virtue that they may be repeatedly filled, emptied and moved without the fear of leaks developing – which is very contrary to the case of the old putty-glazed angle-iron tanks.

The beginner should not start with anything smaller than a 90l (20 gals) aquarium – of which the dimensions are 90cm × 30cm × 38cm (36in × 15in × 12in) – as smaller tanks are more difficult to maintain and the proportional setting-up costs are greater. Indeed, the larger the tank the easier it is to maintain. Even the basic 90l (20 gals) aquarium will weigh well over 100kg (220lb) when filled, and so clearly needs to be placed upon a strong base. While the construction of the stand can be a do-it-yourself job of timber or concrete blocks, most aquarists look for a ready-made item. There are a number of strong – and often attractive – metal stands, and an increasing number of cabinet aquaria which aspire towards being pieces of furniture. Lightweight modern cabinets and wall shelves are not strong enough to carry filled aquaria.

Whatever stand is used, it is essential that it is level. If an all-glass tank is chosen then a piece of 1cm (½in) board should be laid on the stand and a layer of expanded polystyrene (such as is used for ceiling tiles) put between this and the base of the tank. This will enable the strain caused by any irregularity in the stand or the floor to be absorbed by the timber and foam and not to be transmitted to the glass. Once the tank is in position check that it is level, using a spirit level, because it will be immovable when filled. Never try to move any tank while it still contains water or gravel. The glass may crack and, as wet glass is very slippery, the tank is easily dropped.

Some form of hood will, in most cases, be needed to house the lighting. This may be made of wood, or plastic or metal units can be bought to fit the standard sizes of tank. If metal is chosen this should be thoroughly painted internally with a non-toxic gloss paint to prevent any condensation running back and possibly carrying toxic metals into the tank.

A plastic condensation trap or cover glass, which fits between the tank and the hood, should also be used. This will cut down on evaporation losses and prevent water splashing the light fittings. Holes may be cut in the plastic sheets, or a corner of the cover glass may be cut off, to allow airlines and heater cables to be run into the tank.

Some thought should be given as to the final siting of the tank. It should be within convenient reach of one or more electrical sockets and should not be positioned where smoke or other pollutant-laden air can be pumped into it. If shy and quiet species of fish are to be housed the tank should not be kept where people will be continually walking past. Unlike freshwater aquaria, a certain amount of green algae growth is desirable for the health of the tank, and so it may be sited where it receives some direct sunlight. This is particularly beneficial when invertebrates are being kept.

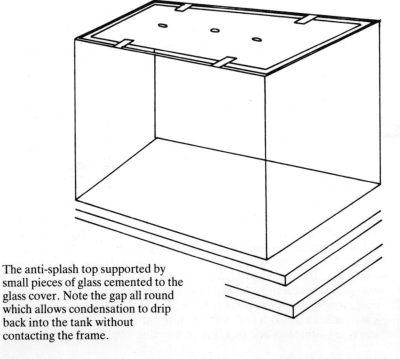

The anti-splash top supported by small pieces of glass cemented to the glass cover. Note the gap all round which allows condensation to drip back into the tank without contacting the frame.

The water

The pioneers among marine tropical fish-keepers did not have the advantage of the ready-mixed salts that are available today. They had to collect their sea-water from the oceans or else make it up themselves from a complex formula of salts and trace elements, that had to be carefully measured. This latter method was at best risky and required the correct use of complex measuring devices. The collection of sea-water, on the other hand, although it might seem to be the simplest method, was also found to be troublesome. The collected water had to be free from pollution and its constitution such that its chemical properties were retained. In practice it was found that it was difficult – due to the presence of organisms that were not wanted – to maintain a balanced environment. In small volumes, the sea-water quickly lost some of its properties and had to be constantly renewed.

Today, we have the benefit of some excellent ready-mixed aquarium salts that, when mixed with the correct volume of water, provide just the right conditions for the maintenance of fish. It is in fact the ideal clean substitute for natural sea-water. There are a number of synthetic sea-salts available, but it is very important to use one which contains a large proportion of the trace elements which occur in natural sea-water and, just as important, to use one which has these in the correct amounts. New artificial sea-water should be mixed in a clean glass or food-grade plastic container. This is then aerated for twenty-four hours or until the salts are thoroughly dissolved and the pH (see page 18) is up to acceptable levels. The specific gravity can then be checked with the hydrometer, making sure the sample tested is at the same temperature as that to which the hydrometer is calibrated. If the specific gravity is too low then more dry salt is added, and if it is too high the salt solution is diluted with more tap-water.

At this stage the water is now ready to maintain marine life but it is vital that efficient filtration is available otherwise the water will soon become polluted and the fish will die. It is here that the confusion between mature water and a biologically matured aquarium arises. Twenty-four-hour-old water is matured, in the sense of being ready for fish, but a tank is not mature until its filter system is capable of dealing with the waste products emitted by its inhabitants.

Water chemistry

Natural sea-water is an extremely complex solution and there are many large volumes dealing with its chemistry. While these contain much of interest for the advanced hobbyist the following brief outline describes the basics which should be understood by all newcomers to the hobby.

Specific gravity The specific gravity of water is its density, determined by the salts dissolved in it. The specific gravity of marine aquarium water can be checked with a suitable hydrometer to ensure that the concentration of salts is at the correct level. Most natural sea-water has a specific gravity (S.G.) of 1.020–1.022. Caribbean water is usually denser, at about 1.025, and Red Sea water can give a measurement as high as 1.035. Fish are adapted to the S.G. prevailing in the waters in which they are found, but if maintained at slightly lower levels their metabolic rate is reduced, they eat less and their life span can be extended. When adding water to the tank to make up for evaporation use warm tap-water only, since *only* water is lost by evaporation. Do not use salt-water as this will result in a steady rise in S.G.

pH The pH scale, from 0–14, is a logarithmic scale measuring the acidity or alkalinity of the water. A level of 7 is neutral while a reading below this is acidic, and above it alkaline. Natural sea-water has a pH of around 8.1–8.3 and this should be matched in the aquarium. Freshly made-up synthetic sea-water has a pH of around 8.3 but as all the fishes' waste products are acidic this will tend to fall. Buffer solutions, to maintain the correct pH, should be used regularly along with partial water changes of about 25 percent every two months. Most fish can slowly be acclimatised to a pH of 7.9–8.0 but high pH levels, over 8.4, should be avoided as there is an increased risk of ammonia poisoning.

Trace elements Almost every naturally occurring element has been found in sea-water, at greater or lesser concentrations, and the best synthetic salt mixes include a large number of these in their formulations. Those chemicals found in very small quantities are called trace-elements. While many probably are unimportant as far as the fish are concerned, equally many have been shown to be vitally important. The fish, invertebrates and plants absorb these trace elements and use them for growth, reproductive and metabolic processes. The trace element level in aquarium water can be maintained at correct levels with the use of a trace element booster solution or by very regular partial water changes (10–20 percent per month).

Nitrogen cycle Fishes' waste products are poisonous to them, and the nitrogen cycle is nature's way of breaking down wastes and recycling them into safe and beneficial re-usable end products. In the aquarium the nitrogen cycle is essentially as follows: wastes from the animals (urea, excreta, etc.) are converted first to ammonia (extremely toxic), then to nitrites (very toxic) and then to nitrates (marginally toxic at high concentrations). The nitrates are used as fertiliser by the algae which are in turn eaten by the fish to complete the cycle. Establishing a working nitrogen cycle in the aquarium is vitally important, but achieved easily with an efficient undergravel filter. When the nitrogen cycle is working the tank is said to have 'matured' and is then ready to house fish.

Stability The coral reefs are probably the world's most stable environments. There is never any great variation in temperature, S.G., pH or chemical composition, and very little pollution. Because of this the fish do not have the adaptability of freshwater fish which have to survive more varying conditions. In the aquarium this means that all environmental changes should be made very slowly. However, the effort of keeping water conditions at optimal levels is well rewarded. Clearly small volumes of water will tend to undergo adverse chemical changes more rapidly than larger volumes, and it is for this reason that beginners are advised to start with tanks of at least 90l (20 gals) capacity. Additionally, small tanks tend to encourage overstocking which is very dangerous. The maximum stocking level allowable is 2.5cm (1in) of fish for every 9l (2 gals) of water; in fact it is preferable to stock at 2.5cm (1in) to every 13.6l (3 gals) for the first six months of the tank's life.

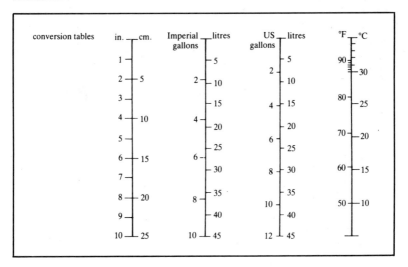

Use the tables for any conversions of sizes, quantities or temperatures you may wish to make.

Filtration and aeration

The provision of an efficient filtration system is one of the most important factors in the successful maintenance of marine aquaria. Filtration serves two major purposes: it removes suspended particulate matter from the field of view, and it breaks this (and dissolved, harmful chemicals) down into harmless end products. The former is generally called 'mechanical filtration' and the latter 'biological filtration'. A good filter system will perform both functions at the same time.

Mechanical filtration works by pulling the water through a fine medium, such as filter-wool or fine gravel, which prevents the return of debris to the water. Biological filtration is the conversion, by *Nitrosomas* and *Nitrobacter* bacteria, of the animals' waste products and is achieved by passing the polluted, but well-aerated, water through a filter medium containing these bacteria. In most circumstances the newcomer to the hobby would be advised to use the normal, or the reverse-flow, undergravel systems.

The undergravel filter The simplest and most cost-effective method of achieving these twin aims is with the sub-sand or undergravel filters. These have been proved reliable and effective over many years and can be used successfully in any size of tank. They comprise a perforated plastic plate that rests about 1cm (½in) off the bottom of the aquarium. An air lift connected to this plate causes water to be pulled from beneath it. More water then flows down through the substrate (the sand or gravel) to replace it. This flow of water draws with it any suspended matter, or dissolved chemicals, into the gravel where it is quickly broken down into a harmless humus by bacterial action. The grain size and depth of the substrate is important; it should be between 2 and 3mm (about ⅛in) in diameter and at least 8cm (about 3in) deep. A mixture of crushed cockle shell and coral sand, in the ratio of 1:2 is ideal. If undergravel filters are used the only additional filtration necessary will be the inclusion of one or more small box filters, of the type familiar to freshwater aquarists, which is filled with high activity marine grade charcoal.

Power filters Another successful, but considerably more expensive, means of filtration, is by the use of electrically operated power filters. These comprise a motor unit which pulls water through a canister containing, when used for marine aquaria, charcoal and coral sand. These filters have the advantage of being more easily cleaned than undergravel filters and of eliminating the bubbling action which attends undergravel filters. However, whatever type of filter is used it must be capable of moving the tank's entire water volume at least three times an hour, and should include a large culture of nitrifying bacteria. The number of these bacteria is directly related to the available solid surfaces upon which they can grow. Clearly, an undergravel filter which uses coral sand, etc., will have a greater surface area on which the bacteria can grow than will the canister of all but the very largest power filters, and will thus promote a greater growth of nitrifying bacteria. Systems which depend upon power filters rather than an undergravel filter are often known as sterile-system tanks. Such tanks are usually equipped with ozonisers, protein skimmers and occasionally ultra-violet steriliser units.

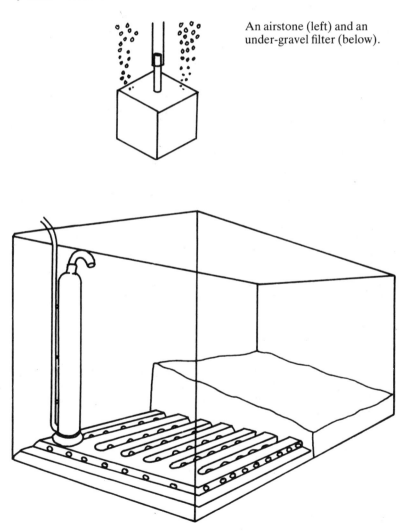

An airstone (left) and an under-gravel filter (below).

Charcoal is used in both systems to remove those chemical pollutants which cannot be broken down by bacterial activity.

Combination systems An increasingly popular system, and one which combines the virtues of both power and undergravel filters, is the reverse-flow undergravel system. Here, water is drawn from the tank into a power filter where it first goes through filter-wool and then charcoal. The water is then pumped under an undergravel filter plate from where it is pushed up through the substrate back into the body of the tank. This greatly reduces the build-up of humus in the gravel, debris being sucked directly into the power filter from where it is easily removed. It retains the large nitrifying filter-bed of the normal undergravel filter and, in addition, is very quiet to operate.

Other systems Undergravel filtered tanks are generally called semi-natural systems. Another alternative is the natural system. This is mainly of interest to aquarists wishing to keep mainly invertebrates (animals without backbones) and should not be attempted by inexperienced hobbyists. In this method filtration is left to the filter-feeding invertebrates, such as sponges and feather-duster worms, with only mild aeration being provided to give a little water movement. Nitrification of harmful chemicals is dependant on those comparatively few bacteria which develop on rocks and the surface of a very thin layer of coral sand which comprises the substrate. When used successfully the natural system is very attractive but it will only house a very few fish and, if over-loaded, is rapidly polluted. No more than one 2.5cm (1in)-long fish should be allowed for each 36l (8 gals) of a natural system. This compares with the 2.5cm (1in) of fish to 9l (2 gals) maximum allowed in either sterile or semi-natural system tanks.

A new and fairly revolutionary filter system has recently been introduced. Here, a motor unit sucks water through a sponge, to remove particulate matter, and then a proportion is directed through canisters suspended above the water, which contain a very porous synthetic gravel, where nitrification takes place. While technically very sophisticated this system is expensive, particularly as aquarists are also advised to use its matching high-powered protein skimmer.

Aeration The filtration system normally supplies sufficient oxygen into the tank by its own action. Where additional oxygen or water movement is required, an airstone can be incorporated into the tank, operated by the filter pump or by a separate pump.

Heating and lighting

Heating The tropical marine aquarium will need to be kept at a temperature of between 24–26.5 deg C (75–80 deg F). This temperature range is adequate for most aquarium fish and invertebrates, with only very few needing a higher or lower level. The temperature should not be allowed to fluctuate more than 1–2 degrees within twenty-four hours or the fish may suffer from one of the stress related diseases. To achieve this a reliable heater and thermostat unit is required. Heating pads on which the tank can be stood are the most inconspicuous heaters but these are expensive and usually a separate thermostat unit has to be purchased.

The most popular form is the combined heater and thermostat unit. This looks like a large test tube, containing a heating element at the end and either a solid-state or a flexible, bi-metallic strip thermostat at the top. This should not be laid horizontally in the tank but may otherwise be positioned at any angle and so can easily be hidden behind rocks, corals, etc. Combined units are plugged directly into the mains supply and should not be fitted with on-off switches as inadvertent cooling may result. Contrary to most manufacturers' instructions a 100 watt unit will prove sufficient for a 90l (20 gals) nett tank, and a 200 watt unit will be enough for a 205l (45 gals) aquarium unless the tanks are sited in particularly cold positions. Most thermostats contain a small light which glows when the water is being heated. Heaters should never be switched on unless they are in water, and must not be removed from the tank when hot, or damage to the unit may occur.

Each aquarium should have at least one thermometer which should be checked several times a day to give early warning of heater or thermostat failure. The most accurate types are filled with mercury but these must be used very carefully as any spillage of mercury into the tank will quickly poison the inhabitants. The most popular types are those filled with alcohol, and the newer liquid crystal digital thermometers. The latter are slightly more expensive but are very easy to read and more accurate than alcohol thermometers.

Lighting Correct lighting is one of the least appreciated factors in the effort to produce a successful and aesthetically pleasing marine aquarium. If fish only are to be kept, then comparatively low levels of light intensity are sufficient; two full-length fluorescent tubes over a 30cm (12in) wide tank being adequate to show the fish to advantage and to produce a minimal growth of green algae. This algae growth is important in providing a necessary food source for members of the Acanthuridae and many Chaetodontidae.

However, if a good range of invertebrate animals (anemones, living corals, etc.) is to be successfully maintained then the aquarium must be lit much more brightly. If fluorescent tubes are to be used then an allowance of 30 watts per square foot (929 sq cm) of water surface should be provided.

While intensity of light is important the correct colour of light matters equally. There are a number of makes of tubes which approximate to natural daylight, all of which may be used. Coloured tubes are available but should be considered as supplemental light rather than the main source.

A very good light source, of comparatively recent introduction to the hobby, is the colour-corrected, cold, mercury vapour light. This gives a very intense light, of correct colour, with little heat; however, it is difficult to incorporate into the standard designs of aquarium hood. These lights are normally suspended, pendant-fashion, over tanks which have just a protective sheet of glass between the water and the light. Until mercury vapour lights are reduced in price most aquarists will continue to use fluorescent tubes, and the provision of some form of hood over the tank, to hold the tubes and reflect the light downwards, will be necessary. Most commercially available hoods are made of sheet aluminium, although some fibreglass and wooden models are also available. It is worth repeating that any metal lid sited over a marine tank must be given at least two coats of a non-toxic gloss paint on the internal surfaces, and should be protected from water splash and condensation by plastic or glass sheeting between it and the water surface. A better answer is to make a wooden hood. The advent of laminate-faced blockboard in a wide range of sizes makes this a very simple proposition.

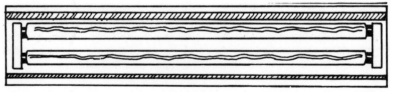

Underside view of tank cover showing fluorescent lighting – an increasingly popular method of providing even illumination.

Other equipment

There are a number of pieces of equipment which may be offered to the marine aquarist apart from the obviously necessary heaters, air pumps, lights, etc. These include the diatom filter, ozoniser, protein skimmer and ultra-violet steriliser. While none of these items is essential, all of them can serve a useful function at certain times. It must not be thought that the beginner will not make a success of the hobby if he does not have these expensive accessories.

Diatom filters are basically the same as a standard power filter except that instead of using filter-wool and charcoal as the filter medium they use powdered diatomaceous earth. This has the ability to filter out particles as small as one micron (the millionth part of a metre), which means this type of filter can actually strain out many disease organisms from the aquarium water. This can be very useful if the aquarist does not want to add any medications to the tank for one reason or another. Unfortunately diatom filters cannot be run continuously because, owing to the fineness with which they filter, they soon become clogged and the water flow is cut to a trickle.

Ozoniser This is an electrical item which, by generating a high-powered spark, produces ozone which is dispersed into the tank through a fine-bubble diffuser. Ozone is a strong oxidising agent and is useful for curing and restricting the spread of bacterial and fungal infections. The claims made for ozone curing a wide range of parasitic infections appear to have been overstressed, however. Ozone has also been implicated in the formation of cancers, and so should be used with care and at a low rate if it is to be used continuously.

Protein skimmer This somewhat ungainly piece of apparatus can serve a very useful purpose, particularly in tanks which house a lot of fish, or fish like groupers and triggers which tend to produce a great deal of waste products. The principles on which protein skimmers work are fairly complex, but their action is simple. By passing a stream of fine bubbles through a column of polluted water a foam is generated at the top. The foam traps a great deal of organic matter and the design of the skimmer is such that this foam is removed from the tank, usually into a plastic cup which the aquarist empties at regular intervals. An efficient skimmer will remove a surprising amount of unwanted material. By using an ozoniser to produce the bubbles the efficiency of the skimmer can be increased by up to 300 percent.

Ultra-violet steriliser This is used in conjunction with a water pump or power filter. The steriliser comprises an ultra-violet light source around which water is pumped. An opaque outer jacket prevents the light damaging fish or human eyes. Ultra-violet light is a powerful sterilising agent and a very effective bacteriocide, but it seems doubtful that aquarium models are as efficient as claimed. The problem is the conflict between the length of time an organism must be exposed to ultra-violet light to be killed, and the need to move a large proportion of the tank water past the light source as quickly as possible.

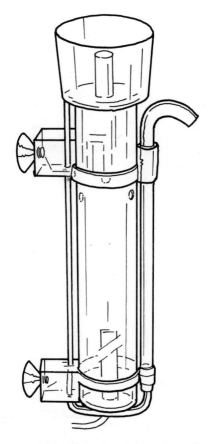

Protein skimmers are useful pieces of equipment in tanks which house many fish, or with fish which produce large quantities of waste.

Setting-up the aquarium

There is nothing complicated or magical about successfully starting a marine aquarium, and the following guidelines should enable anyone to do so. Assuming the beginner is starting with a 90l (20 gals) tank, it must be remembered that this will weigh well over 100kg (220lb) when full and running. The tank must be positioned on a strong, level and stable surface. Place the undergravel filter on the base of the tank and erect the air lift. The filter-plate should cover the whole of the base. A 2.5cm (1in) layer of washed cockle shell is then placed on the filter plate. This is followed by a 5–7.5cm (2–3in) layer of washed coral sand. Connect the air lift to a suitable air pump, but do not switch it on. The pump should be capable of delivering about 300 litres of air per hour. Run water from the cold tap to waste for five or ten minutes and then, using a clean bucket of known volume, begin filling the tank, pouring carefully onto a saucer or dish placed in the tank to avoid disturbing the

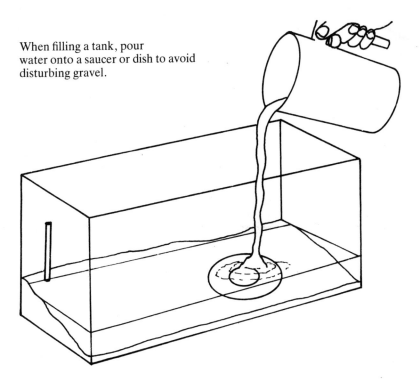

When filling a tank, pour water onto a saucer or dish to avoid disturbing gravel.

sand. When the tank is half full add the contents of a 90l (20 gals) bag of synthetic sea-salts. Continue filling until the water level is 2.5cm (1in) from the top of the tank. Now make a note of the water volume for future reference when using medications or water additives.

Place the heater-thermostat unit in the tank and connect it to the mains supply. The air pump can now be switched on. The water will slowly warm and water will be seen issuing from the filter air lift. Put the thermometer in a place where it can be read easily, but is not obtrusive.

After twenty-four hours the salt will be fully dissolved and the water up to temperature. Adjust the thermostat if the temperature is too high or if it has switched the heater off while the temperature is still low. Check the specific gravity of the water with a hydrometer designed for aquarium purposes. If the water is too dense remove some from the tank and replace with cold tap-water to dilute the salt-water. If the specific gravity is low then add more dry sea-salts and recheck when this is fully dissolved.

When the temperature and specific gravity are correct, tank decor can be added if required (see page 19). Begin to add one of the commercially available maturation fluids according to the instructions provided. This will stimulate the growth of the vital nitrifying bacteria prior to fish being introduced. After three or four daily additions, begin daily tests with a nitrite test kit. Continue adding maturation fluid until the nitrite test gives a reading of about 15 parts per million (ppm), and then stop. Carry on with the nitrite tests daily until a reading of 0ppm is achieved. At this stage there are sufficient bacteria to deal with the wastes from the fish which are soon to be introduced. Next, carry out a pH test. If the reading is between 8.1 and 8.3 then one or two small fish may be added to the tank. If the reading is lower than this then a 25 percent water change, using new sea-water made up to the manufacturer's instructions, must be made. Another pH test will then show the reading to be raised and the tank is then ready for fish.

This maturation period normally takes about two weeks, but may be considerably accelerated by leaving the lights on throughout and by adding a few kilograms of gravel from an existing tank at the 15ppm nitrite stage.

The tank is now 'matured' and ready for livestock. A charcoal filter should now be included, and regular additions of pH buffer solution, trace element and vitamin supplement and algal fertiliser made. Bi-monthly 25 percent water changes and regular removal of waste food and debris will keep the tank in good condition.

Decorating the tank is normally done before the maturing process begins, but if 'living-rock' is to be used this should wait until the tank is fully mature. Final adjustments to the decor should be made before fish are introduced to avoid upsetting them unduly. If water is removed from the tank to make way for rocks and corals, then the revised contents should be noted.

Decor

Salt-water is a very corrosive substance and any article which is considered for inclusion in a marine aquarium must be chemically stable or at least must not produce any harmful effects. This precludes many attractive rocks which can safely be used in freshwater aquaria. Of the many types of stone available the best are the hard limestones, such as Westmoreland, and the softer, cream coloured tuffa. A wide range of shells is available and also the very attractive dead corals. Any rocks to be used should be well scrubbed in clean water, to remove soil, etc. Westmoreland is cheaper but tuffa has the advantage of being soft enough to saw or chisel into decorative shapes.

Shells are available in two forms, either as univalves (whelks, conchs, etc.), or as bivalves (clams, oysters, etc.). Most shells are sold as 'cleaned', and bivalve shells can easily be checked. When dealing with univalves it is good practice to drill a hole in the pointed end as traces of the dead shellfish are often left behind and can then be removed. The introduction of rotting shellfish to the tank is one of the most common and serious ways of polluting the tank.

Carefully positioned corals will enhance your tank.

A wide variety of dead coral skeletons is available. The vast majority are white, but there is also the red organ pipe coral *(Tubipora)*, and a pale blue type which forms sheets or massive pieces. Any other types which are coloured have been dyed and may either fade in the tank or, more seriously, cause poisoning. Again most will have been bleached. If not, then the coral is soaked for a week in a bleach solution of one cupful to 4.5l (1 gal) of water. In either case the coral must be rinsed until there is no residual smell of chlorine. Other attractive natural items include the sea-whips and sea-fans, which are well described by their names. These are the skeletons of various soft corals and are very difficult to make fit for inclusion in the tank. They often appear red, pink or yellow but this coloured layer must be removed to reveal the horny brown-black structure before they are safe. This can be achieved by repeated bleaching in a double strength solution.

Most plastic plants designed for freshwater aquaria are safe for marine use and, if you wish to include them, most plastic ornaments can also be included.

While all the aforementioned items must be rigorously cleaned before use the best rocks for marine aquaria are far from sterile. These are the lumps of rock taken from tropical rock-pools and reef edges and which are generally known as 'living rock'. These pieces of calcareous rock are clad with algae and house many varied animals, often including small crabs, shrimps and shellfish as well as many micro-organisms. All these help create a more balanced environment which is particularly appreciated by invertebrates. Living rock without doubt gives the most natural appearance, but has the drawback of being very expensive.

If you wish to add decorative algae – as opposed to that which should be encouraged to develop naturally – it should be added before the fish are introduced, to avoid disturbing them.

Buying your fish

When purchasing a fish you should look for a specimen that shows erect fins, bright colours and has a well-fed look. Avoid fish that have sunken bellies or those that constantly rub themselves against corals or rocks; this could be a sign of irritation caused by the presence of disease. If any of the occupants of the tank look sick, then beware, it is likely that all the fish are carriers even though the disease may not be in evidence in all the fish in the tank. When purchasing for the first time do not be persuaded to buy species about which you know nothing. It is better to go out with the intention of buying specific species that are known to be compatible. Try to buy locally – the journey home will be shorter and the shock to the fish much reduced. Take a polystyrene lined box with you to retain heat in the polythene water bag. Avoid unnecessary jarring and vibration and handle your captives like eggs. Choose specimens that are bright and active, that are clean-looking and can be seen to be eating. Before leaving the store get as much information as you can. Find out how long they have had the fish, at what S.G. and temperature it was being kept at, where it came from, whether it is feeding satisfactorily and what it is eating. Observe whether it appears aggressive towards other fish or whether it has territorial inclinations. It is far better to make a preliminary sortie to the store on a fact finding mission. Speak to the owner about your intending purchases, most are delighted to discuss all aspects of marine fishkeeping with intended purchasers, after all you may well be a regular customer of theirs in the future and will almost certainly patronise the store that gives a personal and informed service. On the other hand you should beware of the dealer who is not prepared to spend time in discussion with you. There are some dealers whose knowledge is not what it should be; their only target is to make a sale, and as quickly as possible before the badly kept fish die in their tanks. Fortunately these dealers are in the minority and their policy is a short-sighted one as a buyer 'once bitten is twice shy' of returning to that store again. If you follow the principle of good purchasing and go out to buy only specific species for which you have planned a home and for which you have the right food to hand then you should not encounter any problems that cannot be solved by careful maintenance. Good beginners' fish are gobies, blennies, cardinal fish, and some types of anemone fish (clownfish), wrasses and damsel fish.

When you return home with your purchases, they should be introduced to their new environment gradually. The room lights should be dimmed, the tank lights switched off. The polythene bag containing the fish should be floated in the water to allow the temperatures to even up. Remember to open the top of the bag or the fish may suffer from lack of oxygen. Allow the water in the bag to mix gradually with the tank water; this will avoid any sudden change which might occur if the pH factors or S.G. vary. Newly introduced fish usually seek the shelter of coral and they should be left alone for some hours after which they may be coaxed from their cover by offering tempting morsels of food. Any food lying uneaten should be syphoned from the tank to avoid pollution. Remember to drop the food over a clear spot in the tank so that it can easily be removed if necessary.

Remember, finally, that the majority of fish will acclimatise well provided that your tank is mature and ready for them.

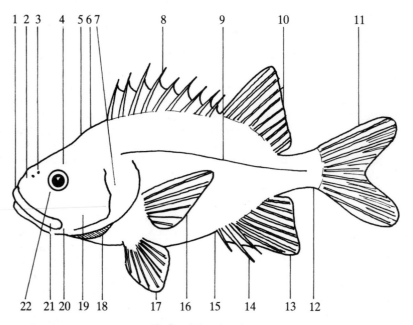

1 Premaxillary	12 Caudal peduncle
2 Snout	13 Anal fin
3 Nostrils	14 Spiny anal fin
4 Interorbital space	15 Anus
5 Occiput	16 Pectoral fin
6 Nape	17 Pelvic fin
7 Opercular lid	18 Gill membranes
8 Spiny dorsal fin	19 Preopercle
9 Lateral line	20 Isthmus
10 Soft dorsal fin	21 Maxillary
11 Caudal fin	22 Suborbital region

Feeding

Once the environmental and water constitution problems have been overcome the final problem is to provide food of the right types in the right quantity and to ensure that it is eaten. Providing the right food in the right quantity is the most difficult problem. In their natural habitat fish have a wide choice of food available at any one time and it is probable that they vary their diet to some extent. The quantity and variety of food to which they are accustomed, if introduced into the aquarium would soon pollute the water, and so some choice has to be made by the aquarist as to which foods to feed to his fish.

Do not overfeed, as uneaten food can easily cause pollution. The correct amount to give can only be gauged by observation over a period of time. Uneaten food left lying at the bottom after the first few minutes' feeding may well be taken by more docile species after the aggressive feeders have had their fill. It is important to ensure that each fish gets its share, just as it is important to see that food is not left uneaten. As the marine hobby becomes more popular so an increasing range of foods is available to the hobbyists' fish. The best foods are the specialised dried foods for marine fish together with the very wide range of irradiated frozen foods. Prior to irradiated foods becoming available many aquarists bought their fish foods from fishmongers, but this is no longer necessary and certainly no live, or uncooked sea-derived food should be introduced to the tank for fear of introducing disease. Of the live foods available only *Artemia* (brine shrimp) and earthworms may be considered safe. As a general rule only use live foods when particularly demanded by fish or invertebrates which are reluctant to take prepared foods.

In the wild many fish are grazers or opportunist feeders, eating what they can as they find it and so clearly a diet, in captivity, of one type of frozen food is not going to prove satisfactory. Algae should be promoted in the tank, by the use of algal fertilisers and good lighting, to provide fresh vegetable matter. Further vegetable matter can be supplied by chopped spinach leaves or vegetable dried foods. Any fish which will take dried foods should be given it, as the major brands include a wide variety of foods in the mix. A range of three or four frozen foods should be given in rotation. Two feeds per day – one being with dried food – is usually sufficient but young fish will benefit from more but smaller feeds. The regular addition of an aquarium vitamin solution will benefit both fish and invertebrates.

Diseases

Like all other animals, marine fish are subject to a number of bacterial, parasitic, fungal and viral diseases. Fortunately only a few are at all common and with the recent advances in aquarium technology most can be successfully treated or avoided. Provided marine fish are housed properly, given a good diet and sensible water management they appear to be intrinsically more hardy than many freshwater species. This would appear to be mainly due to two factors. Firstly, when the tank conditions are suitable for one marine fish, they are usually suitable for the vast majority; this is by no means the case with tropical freshwater fish. Secondly, salt-water contains many fewer bacteria and fungal organisms than freshwater, and in itself has certain bacteriocidal properties.

Many books have, in the past, advocated the use of broad spectrum antibiotics as wonder cure-alls for many marine fish diseases. Unless a separate quarantine tank is available these should not be used by the amateur. In no circumstances should they be used in the display aquarium as they will kill the vital nitrifying bacteria upon which the breakdown of toxic waste products in the tank depends.

One of the most difficult tasks regarding marine fish diseases is making the correct diagnosis, and here the help and advice of an experienced pet shop owner will be found invaluable. The following brief guidelines should enable the beginner to recognise and success-fully treat the commonest diseases. In most instances preparations can be added to the tank directly. Adhere rigidly to the manufacturer's instructions.

Oodinium This is a parasitic infection where a microscopic organism invades the gills and skin. The symptoms are very rapid breathing, lethargy, reluctance to feed and, in its latter stages, a grey or brown film which covers the body. This disease is very contagious and usually quickly fatal if left untreated because it causes major gill tissue damage. Oodinium is easily cured with commercially available che-lated copper sulphate solutions. Oodinium, and indeed many other fish diseases, is often termed as 'stress-induced'; that is, resulting from some environmental change on a scale with which the fish is not equipped to deal. Nitrite poisoning, chilling and long-term persecution by other fish commonly give rise to oodinium infections.

White-spot The name of this disease describes its external appearance very well. Infected fish appear to be liberally covered with white, or grey, salt granules. Again, massive damage is done to the gills but it is

easily treated with chelated copper sulphate if caught in time
oodinium, there is no guaranteed effective cure which can be s
used in the mixed fish and invertebrate system. Any increase in cop
levels in the water, above what is naturally found, is extremely toxic
invertebrate animals and also to sharks and rays.

Flukes This is the common name given to a number of small worm-like
parasites which occasionally infest marine and freshwater fish. These
may infect the body, where they show as blurred white spots (particularly in the fins), or the gills, or both. Typically the fish will swim in a
jerky fashion, repeatedly scratch against rocks and may have very
laboured breathing. It may even shut down one gill chamber. It is best
to use one of the commercially available treatments specifically designed to meet this problem. The new generation of chemicals seem
particularly safe and effective. Infections of flukes are particularly
common in spring and autumn, where unsterilised foods have been
used, and in dirty aquaria.

Bacterial problems These are fortunately few and far between in
correctly maintained aquaria. Most bacterial problems are associated
with damaged fish and so tend to appear most commonly among newly
imported or purchased fish, or among those which fight among themselves. Typically, infected fish show reddened or greyish areas on the
bodies and fins. There are a number of effective treatments available,
many of which can safely be used in tanks housing invertebrates. It is
good policy to use one of these for a few days whenever a new fish is
introduced to the tank, as some are very good all-purpose preventa-
tives.

Fungus There appear to be comparatively few fungal organisms
affecting marine fish and only very rarely are these contagious. External thread-like fungus sometimes appears where fish have been injured
but this can normally be cured with chelated copper sulphate. The
most serious fungus infecting marine fish is one which develops
internally, called *Ichthyosporidium hoferi*. Although rare it sometimes
appears, particularly among *Centropyge* species. *I. hoferi* infection
usually produces bulging eyes and abnormal swelling of the abdomen.
There is no effective cure and infected fish should be destroyed.

Viral diseases Lymphocystis is the commonest viral infection likely to
be encountered. This appears like small cauliflower growths on damaged fins and body tissue. It will usually heal of its own accord, given
good food and proper care, but occasionally becomes chronic. Infected fin tissue can be surgically removed with a sharp scalpel.
Alternatively, the nascent oxygen preparations available have pro-
duced some good results.

Pop-eye Although fairly common, this is not so much a disease in its own right as a common symptom of a number of problems. As the name suggests one or both eyes will protrude from the socket. Pop-eye is most commonly seen among *Amphiprion* species, as well as greedy but messy feeders such as groupers and triggerfish. In extreme cases eyes may be lost. Clearly the basic problem, which may vary from internal fungus to metal poisoning, needs to be attended to but the following first aid often results in the swelling subsiding and avoids the disfigurement of the fish. Change a quarter of the tank water, then do not feed or illuminate the tank for the next four days. Often at the end of this time the eye will be back to normal.

There are many other diseases which may strike at some time. All marine aquarists should include at least one good book about diseases in their library and keep a first aid kit of a few selected commercial medications ready for when needed. Having said this it should be stressed that fish are innately hardy and most diseases, particularly among established stock, are due to the aquarist's negligence over such matters as water quality, diet and other stress-producing factors.

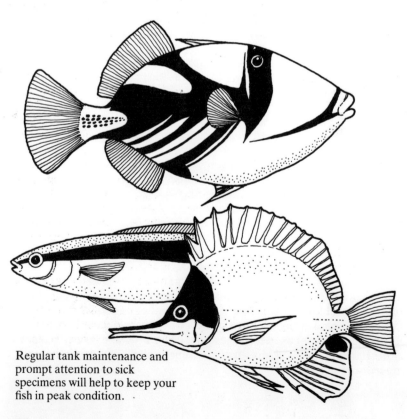

Regular tank maintenance and prompt attention to sick specimens will help to keep your fish in peak condition.

Invertebrates

One of the most fascinating aspects of the marine hobby, and one which is increasingly popular, is the keeping of invertebrate animals. This group, the animals without backbones, includes such varied creatures as sea-anemones, shrimps, urchins and oysters. Many are brilliantly coloured, have interesting habits and are easy to maintain in the home aquarium.

Invertebrates are so diverse that some can be found for almost any situation. Some want intense lighting, others prefer it subdued, some are active scavengers or predators while others quietly filter minute particles of food from the water. Clearly some care must be taken when selecting invertebrates to ensure that conditions are generally suitable, that they will not eat or be eaten by the fish, or indeed, that they will not eat each other. A huge range is available with more being seen each year. The advice of a reputable dealer is invaluable when selecting. Special foods can be purchased for those species which will not take standard fish foods.

Crustaceans This group includes the crabs, lobsters, shrimps and barnacles. Many shrimps are brightly coloured in red and white, all are excellent scavengers and in the wild a number will pick parasites from fish in the same manner as the cleaner wrasse. Of the crabs, the most popular are the hermit crabs, which make their homes in the discarded shells of univalve molluscs, and the arrow crabs, which have an arrow-head shaped body supported by spider-like legs. Lobsters and the clawless spiny lobsters are available which are red, blue or green. Many of these, however, grow quite large, and need correspondingly large aquaria. All large crabs and lobsters can be destructive and may catch and eat small fish. Certain small species of shrimps and crabs make their home in the tentacles of sea-anemones, in the same manner as *Amphiprion* species of clownfish. Two species which should be rigidly excluded from the mixed aquarium are mantis shrimps and swimming crabs – both of which are voracious predators.

The bodies of crustaceans are supported by a rigid external skeleton which is shed periodically to enable a sudden spurt of growth before the new shell hardens. The frequency of shedding depends on how well fed the animal is, but may be as often as every two weeks. A pH of 8.2–8.3 is essential as deformities may occur at lower levels. Hermit crabs should be provided with a selection of shells to enable them to move 'home' as they grow.

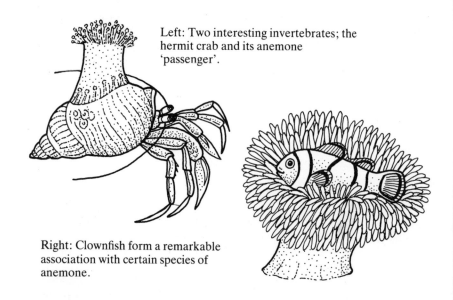

Left: Two interesting invertebrates; the hermit crab and its anemone 'passenger'.

Right: Clownfish form a remarkable association with certain species of anemone.

Echinoderms This group includes the starfish, sea-urchins, sea-cucumbers and the crinoids. Again many of these are highly coloured and, given good conditions, all except the crinoids are quite easy to maintain. Crinoids, though very attractive, are among the most difficult animals to keep for any length of time.

Starfish can, for practical purposes, be divided into two groups. Those with knobs on the arms are generally predatory and will eat quite large pieces of shellfish and fish. Those with smooth arms generally take only small particles such as may be passed over by the fish in the tank.

Sea-urchins are characterised by their near-spherical bodies which are armed with spines of varying thickness. Again, some may damage sessile invertebrates and a number, fortunately rarely seen, have a dangerous venomous capability. However, all are useful scavengers and will eat copious amounts of algae. All species require good water conditions or they will shed their spines and die.

The sea-cucumbers, which vary in size and appearance from large, brown specimens, to very small, brightly coloured ball-shaped animals, all eat fine particles of food. Some ingest sand and mud, digesting the useful organic material and excreting clean sand. The more interesting species, from an aquarium point of view, have feathery tentacles around the mouth which trap small, floating particles of food. The tentacles are then pushed, one by one, into the mouth and in effect sucked clean. When they are alarmed some species will void the internal organs, as a deterrent to aggressors. In the wild these organs are slowly regenerated with the animal being none the worse for the experience.

Crinoids look like starfish with very many arms, each of which looks like a coarse feather – hence the common name of feather-stars. They are very brittle and easily damaged. They feed mainly at night on very small particles. Crinoids have the most beautiful mode of swimming, by serpentine undulations of the arms.

Molluscs This very large group contains thousands of species, only a comparative few of which have any degree of popularity with marine aquarists.

Of the bivalves (two-shelled molluscs) the scallops and clams are the most popular. Both are filter feeding animals, taking in water through one vent and pumping it out of the other after extracting what food is available. Many of the scallops have brightly coloured bodies – particularly the flame scallop from the Caribbean – and rows of light-sensitive eyes. They will actively flee from predators by squirting water from within the body with such force that they glide clumsily around the tank. Clams need intense lighting and plenty of food if they are to prosper.

Among the univalves, the most popular are the cowries. These have ovoid, highly polished shells. They will eat a great deal of algae and some species will damage anemones. Most of the other univalves are predatory and a number – some members of the cone family – have deadly poisonous stings.

The most attractive group of molluscs are undoubtedly the nudibranchs, which have no shells, and which include some of the most colourful animals in the world. Species vary in size from under 1cm to over 30cm (½in to 12in) and come in a variety of colours. Unfortunately they are extremely difficult to keep as most species are very selective in their diet – eating, for example, only one species of sponge or one type of sea-squirt.

This group, besides containing some very attractive animals also includes the most intelligent invertebrates, namely the octopuses and squid. Though fascinating animals to keep they require absolutely optimum conditions and must not be kept with fish or crustaceans as these latter will be eaten. Very shy, the octopuses require plenty of hiding places and the minimum of disturbance. Squid are equally nervous and, being very fast swimmers, often damage themselves on the sides of their aquaria. These animals should only be considered by the experienced aquarist.

Coelenterates Many of the most popular marine invertebrates such as anemones, hard and soft corals, and jellyfish are members of this group.

For aquarium purposes anemones can be divided into two groups: those in which clownfish (*Amphiprion* species) will live, and those which they will not inhabit. The former includes the genera *Radianthus, Stoicactis* and *Discosoma*. These all require high light intensities, must be fed with pieces of fish or shrimp, and will grow to 45cm (18in) or more in diameter. There are white, pink, fawn, blue, purple and green varieties. Fewer types of the non-symbiotic anemones are imported, the most common being the tube-anemones (*Cerianthus* species) and the Caribbean *Condylactis* species. The former has very long fine tentacles and forms a protective tube for its body of mucus and sand. It has a strong sting and commonly catches and eats small fish. *Condylactis* is very easy to keep. They are generally pink or white and have thick fleshy tentacles about 8–12cm (3–5in) long.

Only a very limited range of hard and soft corals is available to the aquarist. Most of these are filter feeding animals taking only small particles of food but a number, among them many of the easier-to-keep species, will take quite large pieces of food. *Plerogyra* (bubble coral) is a notable example. The main requirement for keeping most corals is adequate light. It is almost impossible to provide too much. They all have a high vitamin requirement, require a pH between 8.2 and 8.3 and – soft corals such as gorgonians, alcyonarians and leather corals in particular – appreciate regular feeding with newly hatched brine-shrimp.

Many of the stony corals will survive indefinitely with only the food provided by the algae within their tissue provided the lighting is sufficiently intense.

Very few jellyfish are imported and only the *Cassiopeia* species can be considered good tank inhabitants. Unlike other jellyfish which drift or swim in the mid or top layers of the seas, *Cassiopeia* spends much of its life on the bottom with its feathery tentacles facing upwards. It can be fed on brine shrimp nauplii. *Cassiopeia* is often damaged by fish and other invertebrates, however.

Worms Although this group includes the common earthworm it also includes some very attractive and easy-to-keep marine worms which are very popular among hobbyists. The best-known are the sabellid tubeworms, commonly called feather-dusters. The body is housed in a flexible mucus tube and the mouth is surrounded by a crown of feathery tentacles which may be up to 15cm (6in) in diameter. They are usually available in shades of brown, red, cream and white. They will shed the crown when frightened or reproducing and this should be removed from the tank, but the tube containing the body should be left for a new ring of 'feathers' will be grown. Somewhat less common but equally attractive are the smaller serpulid worms. These produce a hard calcareous tube and are often found embedded in lumps of coral. Rarely more than 1.5cm (⅝in) in diameter serpulids may be white, black, blue, red, yellow or orange. Both families take very fine particles of food but will rapidly withdraw into their protective tubes if disturbed.

Plants

Marine plants, mainly decorative species of algae, have yet to achieve the popularity they deserve. Many aquarists are still dissuaded by the many old books which advise against their use, claiming they are difficult to grow and a potential pollution hazard. If they are treated properly many grow very rapidly and perform a valuable service in fulfilling one stage of the nitrogen cycle.

Marine algae demand high light levels, a good supply of nutrient such as phosphates and nitrates, and of course they suffer if continuously eaten by the fish. Like any other marine organism the plants require proper acclimatisation before introduction to the tank. They should be floated, in a bag, on top of the water for half an hour to accommodate temperature differences, and then the aquarist should spend an hour slowly mixing tank water with that in the bag. Marine plants should never be lifted out of water. The main cause of failure is too rapid a change of specific gravity. This causes the plant cell walls to rupture and the tissue to escape into the water. The algae rapidly pales and dies.

There is an increasing range of algae available to the hobbyist. The easiest to grow are the various *Caulerpa* species, but the various *Penicillus* (merman's shaving brush), *Haliomeda* (sea-cactus) and Ulva *(sea-lettuce)* are none too difficult. Red algae are sometimes available but these are best left to the more experienced hobbyists.

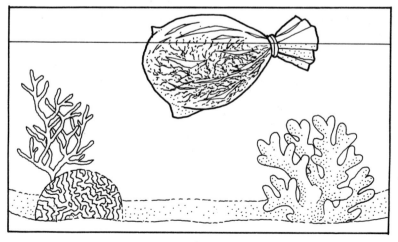

Acclimatise plants by floating them in a bag of water for half an hour.

Aquarium selections

The following selections offer a guide which may be used to achieve an attractive and interesting community display. The fish in each selection are all compatible, but vary in habits and appearance. Unless stated otherwise all specimens are considered small to medium-sized. To the experienced freshwater tropical fish keeper there will seem very few fish per tank, but a surprisingly brilliant display can be created with few fish, particularly as many will be bigger than the standard freshwater community fish. The final choice of fish is a matter of personal taste and availability, so these collections must in no way be considered definitive. With the help of this book and the advice of a knowledgeable fish dealer you should be able to find substitutes comparable in habits and preferences for any of the fish mentioned here should you wish to.

In the descriptive section of fish species, those denoted thus (†) are species which are not recommended for the normal community tank.

Tank size:
24in × 12in × 15in high
(60cm × 30cm × 38cm) – very small tank for only a few fish, but with additional invertebrates

2 *Amphiprion ocellaris*
1 *Stenopus hispidus*
1 *Radianthus* anemone
2 Sabellid worms
1 portion *Caulerpa* spp algae

Tank size:
24in × 12in × 15in high
(60cm × 30cm × 38cm) – very small tank for two small specimen fish which will eventually require a larger tank
1 *Pterois volitans*
1 *Rhineacanthus aculeatus*

Tank size:
36in × 12in × 15in high
(90cm × 30cm × 38cm) – smallest size tank for a beginner. Small to medium-sized fish; lively but peaceful

1 *Chaetodon auriga*
1 *Coris gaimard*
1 *Centropyge flavissimus*
2 *Gobiosoma oceanops*

Tank size:
36in × 12in × 15in high
(90cm × 30cm × 38cm) – very peaceful, small to medium-sized, but fairly demanding species

1 *Lactoria cornutus*
1 *Platax pinnatus*
1 *Gaterin chaetodonoides*
1 *Chelmon rostratus*

Tank size:
36in × 12in × 15in high
(90cm × 30cm × 38cm) – peaceful,
small species and invertebrates

2 *Amphiprion akallopisos*
2 *Hippocampus kuda*
1 *Oxymonacanthus longirostris*
1 *Lythrypnus dalli*
1 *Hippolysmata grabhami*
1 *Discosoma* anemone
1 *Plerogyra* coral
3 Sabellid worms
1 portion each of *Caulerpa* and
Penicillus algae

Tank size:
36in × 12in × 15in high
(90cm × 30cm × 38cm) – boisterous
very hardy fish, some growing quite
large

1 *Abudefduf oxyodon*
1 *Dascyllus aruanus*
1 *Odonus niger*
1 *Canthigaster valentini*
1 *Acanthurus olivaceus*

Tank size:
48in × 15in × 18in high
(120cm × 38cm ×
45cm) – medium-sized, lively and
peaceful fish

1 *Acanthurus lineatus*
1 *Centropyge acanthops*
1 *Centropyge heraldi*
1 *Chaetodon collaris*
1 *Chaetodon vagabundus*
1 *Labroides dimidiatus*
1 *Bolbometopon bicolor*

Tank size:
48in × 15in × 18in high
(120cm × 38cm × 45cm) – larger
fish, more aggressive and with
well-developed characters

1 *Melichthys vidua*
1 *Diodon histrix*
1 *Pterois antennata*
1 *Acanthurus leucosternon*
1 *Bodianus axillaris*

Tank size:
48in × 15in × 18in high
(120cm × 38cm ×
45cm) – community to display one
large show fish to best advantage

1 *Pomacanthus imperator* or
Euxiphipops navarchus
1 *Labroides dimidiatus*
5 *Abudefduf cyanea*
1 *Coris angulata*

Tank size:
48in × 15in × 18in high
(120cm × 38cm × 45cm) – mixed fish
and invertebrate tank with a view to
encouraging fish and invertebrate
spawning

1 pair *Amphiprion clarkii*
1 pair *Abudefduf cyanae*
4 *Gobiosoma oceanops*
1 pair *Hippocampus kuda*
1 pair *Stenopus hispidus*
1 *Stoicactis* anemone
6 Sabellid worms
2 Sea-cucumbers
5 Live corals
1 portion each of *Caulerpa*,
Haliomeda and *Penicillus* algae

Introduction to the fish families

There are many families of fish living in the warmer seas of the world. Many of these have at least a few species which are suitable for the aquarium. In this book representatives from 27 families are briefly described. There should be fish to suit everyone here: large, showy species and small, shy ones; lively, bright fish and some quiet, delicate species; and eye-catching centrepiece fish and less colourful fish but with character.

The family descriptions which follow are intended to give a brief introduction to each family, and the fish chosen for your aquarium may have additional characteristics which a general description cannot fully describe.

Family Acanthuridae

Members of this widespread family are commonly called either surgeon fish or tangs. The common names refer to the sharp, movable spine which is found on both sides of the caudal peduncle and is used when fighting with other fish. These are non-territorial fish of open reefs, and are found in shoals of twenty or more.

Family Apogonidae

This family of fairly small fish is found on reefs throughout the tropics. As their common name of cardinalfish suggests, many species are bright red. They tend to be somewhat shy and retiring, rather slow moving, and make good aquarium fish. They are happiest in tanks with plenty of hiding places.

Family Balistidae

These fish, commonly known as triggerfish, are found in the Atlantic, Pacific and Indian Oceans. The common name derives from the second dorsal spine which unlocks, or triggers the release of, the rigid first dorsal spine. The family all have well-developed teeth. They swim by undulating the soft dorsal and anal fins. They are hardy and long-lived aquarium fish.

Family Blenniidae

Members of this family are found throughout the world. They are small, greedy and essentially carnivorous. They have a tentacle over each eye and are usually found in shallow water and rock pools. They swim poorly – spending much time on the substrate – and are generally hardy aquarium fish.

Family Canthigasteridae

These fish are commonly called puffers because they can inflate the stomach with water or air, as a defence mechanism, when alarmed. Their skin is scalcless, but is rough and prickly. They are slow swimmers, generally peaceful, and are useful scavengers. The Canthigasteridae are found throughout the tropics.

Family Carangidae

Most of this family grow large and many are valuable food fish. Only a few are suitable for aquaria, and then only when small. They are fast swimmers, but are moderately peaceful. Some species are very laterally compressed.

Family Centriscidae

The shrimpfish come from the Indian and Pacific Oceans. They look very unlike fish; the jaws are elongated into a tube, they are very laterally compressed, the tail is an extension of the dorsal fin, and the rear half of the body has the appearance of having been amputated. They swim head-down, often among the spines of sea-urchins. Nervous, peaceful and slow moving, these fish are interesting but difficult to maintain.

Family Chaetodontidae

This family is often divided into two subfamilies: the Chaetodontinae and the Pomacanthinae, which are commonly known as butterflyfish and angelfish respectively. There are some 300 species, among them some of the best-known, most beautiful and most suitable aquarium fish. The butterflyfish tend to be rather delicate but many of the angelfish are quite hardy. The latter are distinguished by having a sharp spine at the base of each gill-plate. Often found in pairs in the wild, most Chaetodontidae are best kept singly in aquaria.

Family Diodontidae

The porcupine puffers are found in the Atlantic, Indian and Pacific Oceans. They become very tame and have well-developed characters. They are easy to keep and generally peaceful. They can inflate the stomach with water when frightened and in this condition give the appearance of a spiky football.

Family Gobiidae

The gobies are characterised, in most species, by having pelvic fins modified to form a weak sucker which assists the fish to hold its position on rocks and seaweeds. Most species are marine but some are found in fresh water. Generally good aquarium fish, a few species have spawned in captivity. They are poor swimmers, spending much time on the bottom.

Family Holocentridae

Known as soldierfish or squirrelfish, many species are bright red but tend to be nocturnal and will eat small fish. Found throughout the tropics they generally prove to be hardy aquarium fish. All species have sharp, stiff spines on the dorsal fin and gill-plates.

Family Labridae

More than 400 species of wrasse are known, some very beautiful. They are found throughout the world, and range in size from just a few inches to several feet long. Many species change colour and sex as they grow. Some wrasse bury themselves in the gravel at night. Most species are omnivorous and make good aquarium fish.

Family Lutjanidae

There are more than 250 species of snappers, most coming from the tropics. Only very few are considered worthy aquarium fish, while the majority are valuable food fish. All are active predators and grow rapidly.

Family Monacanthidae

The filefish or leatherjackets are a relatively little-known family of fish found in all warm seas. Their common names come from the very rough, leathery skin. Most are peaceful but only a few are sufficiently colourful to interest aquarists. They tend to hide among seaweeds when frightened.

Family Monodactylidae

This family contains two regularly seen species, one from the tropical eastern Atlantic and the other from south-east Asia. Both are euryhaline, adapting from sea-water to slightly brackish water with ease. They are lively, comparatively peaceful and easy to keep in aquaria. Both species tend to grow larger in sea-water than in freshwater.

Family Ostraciidae

This family encompasses the boxfish, trunkfish and cowfish. These are some of the most interesting marine fish. They give the impression of being encased within a rigid box-like shell with only the fins, eyes and mouth protruding, and swim slowly and clumsily but without apparent effort. These fish become very tame and many apparently learn to recognise their owners. Unfortunately the boxfish (*Ostracion* species) can emit a toxic mucus if badly frightened and this may kill it and other occupants of the tank.

Family Periophthalmidae

The mudskippers are sometimes considered as a subfamily of the Gobiidae but they show considerable adaptation to allow them to live an amphibious life. They live on mud-flats and mangrove swamps on Atlantic and Indian Ocean coasts, spending much time out of water.

Family Platacidae

The few species of this family are all justifiably popular aquarium fish. Their elongated dorsal and anal fins make them visually appealing, despite generally sombre colours, and they become one of the tamest and most trusting of marine fish. With the exception of one species, they are very hardy and easy to keep.

Family Plectorhynchidae

The four commonly imported members of this family are all brightly coloured and make good aquarium fish. They are docile and efficient scavengers. They are most attractive when young, the adult fish becoming much duller.

Family Pomacentridae

This very large family includes many very popular aquarium fish. Its members are usually split into two groups; the damsel or devil fish and the clown fish. The former are small, lively and very hardy species which live in large aggregations in the wild. Clownfish, which are often red, or orange, and white, live in family groups among the tentacles of sea-anemones which would kill other species of fish.

Family Scaridae

The parrotfish are so called because of their bright colours and their strong teeth which are fused together to form a 'beak'. They are very destructive on the reefs, consuming large quantities of coral. The most colourful specimens are large, adult males and unfortunately only the smaller, less bright juveniles are usually available to the hobbyist.

Family Scatophagidae

This small family of fish is found around the coasts and estuaries of south-east Asia and northern Australia. They live in both brackish and sea-water and are very easy to keep. They will eat almost anything edible as their name, 'hundred-eyed muck-eater', indicates.

Family Sciaenidae

Most members of this family grow too large to interest aquarists but there are three from the Caribbean area which make good, if fast-growing, aquarium fish. Croakers, named for the grunting noises they make, are peaceful and elegant fish. Members of this family have spawned in captivity.

Family Scorpaenidae

The scorpionfish, lionfish and stonefish include some of the most spectacular, most popular and potentially most dangerous of aquarium fish. All are equipped with venomous spines in the dorsal fin and in some species these are potentially lethal. The Scorpaenidae are not aggressive but will eat small fish and crustaceans. Most are crepuscular in the wild but generally become diurnal in captivity. *Pterois* species become quite tame and make a spectacular display.

Family Serranidae

This large family includes some of the giants of the fish world as well as some of the little jewels. All are hardy aquarium fish although many are shy. With the exception of the dwarf species, all are efficient predators and will eat small tank-mates.

Family Syngnathidae

The seahorses and pipefish of the Syngnathidae family are probably the least fish-like of fish. They have no tail fin, but the rear half of the body is prehensile. The seahorse's most unusual feature is that it is the males which give birth to the young.

Family Tetraodontidae

This family includes the fresh and brackish water *Tetraodon* species and the larger, marine *Arothron* species. These can both inflate themselves with air or water for protection. *Arothron* species have strong, sharp teeth and cannot be trusted with small fish or invertebrates. They are slow swimmers and effective scavengers.

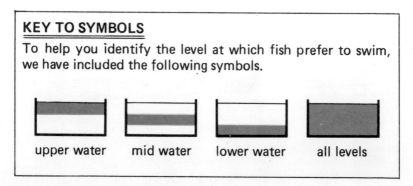

KEY TO SYMBOLS

To help you identify the level at which fish prefer to swim, we have included the following symbols.

upper water   mid water   lower water   all levels

Identification guide

Acanthurus achilles (Acanthuridae)
Common name: Achilles tang,
Red-tailed surgeon
Origin: Hawaii and Mid-Pacific
Size: 20.5cm (8in)
Community tank: Yes, with smaller
species. Provide plenty of open water
for swimming.
Food: Algae, *Artemia, Mysis*, dried
food
SG: 1.020–1.022
Invertebrate compatibility:
Compatible with most, but may
damage serpulid and sabellid worms

Large specimens – over 15cm
(6in) – can be difficult to acclimatise
and require large aquaria. This is one
of the most demanding surgeonfish,
and one which requires perfect water
conditions. It is likely to eat algal
plants placed in the aquarium. The
red spot on the body normally does
not develop until the fish is about 6cm
(2½in) long. An imposing-looking
fish; always ready to display itself,
and very active.

Acanthurus leucosternon
(Acanthuridae)
Common name: Powder blue surgeon
Origin: Sri Lanka, Indian Ocean
Size: 30cm (12in)
Community tank: Yes, but can be aggressive on occasions, particularly towards larger or similar-sized fish. Does not tolerate its own species
Food: Algae, *Artemia, Mysis*, dried food
SG: 1.020–1.022

Invertebrate compatibility: Yes, but may damage holothurians and similar filter-feeding animals

This is one of the most popular surgeonfish but needs good care if it is to thrive. All surgeonfish are grazers, and so a strong growth of algae should be encouraged to provide a continual food source. This species will not tolerate being cramped in small aquaria; a fast and active fish.

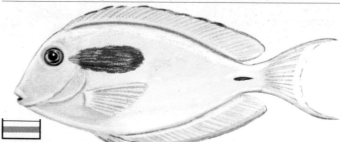

Acanthurus olivaceus
(Acanthuridae)
Common name: Olive surgeon, Shoulder tang
Origin: Mid-Pacific and Australasia
Size: 22cm (8½in)
Community tank: Yes, in large tanks with small fish, but not its own kind
Food: Algae, *Artemia, Mysis*, dried food
SG: 1.020–1.022
Invertebrate compatibility: Yes,

when small – 7.5cm (3in)

One of the easiest surgeonfish to maintain and usually inexpensive to buy. It needs a large tank with strong acration. This species should not be kept with fish larger, or of a similar size, to itself. Like all the Acanthuridae, this species needs a high proportion of vegetable matter in its diet, and will tend to eat aquarium plants.

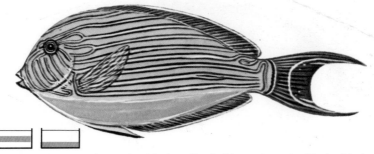

Acanthurus lineatus (Acanthuridae)
Common name: Pyjama tang, Clown surgeon
Origin: Indo-Pacific Ocean
Size: 20.5cm (8in)
Community tank: Yes, one of the most peaceful surgeonfish, but sometimes timid. Although found in small shoals in the wild, none of the *Acanthurus* species will tolerate their own kind in normal sized tanks, however

Food: Algae, *Artemia, Mysis*, dried food
SG: 1.020–1.022
Invertebrate compatibility: Yes

Like all members of the Acanthuridae the colourful-looking pyjama tang has a sharp blade on either side of the caudal peduncle. These can cause severe wounds to other fish and unwary aquarists. Will eat *Caulerpa* and other planted algae.

Naso brevirostris (Acanthuridae)
Common name: Unicorn tang
Origin: Indo-Pacific Ocean
Size: 45cm (18in)
Community tank: Yes, but best when small as the colouring is more interesting
Food: Algae, dried food when young; additional *Artemia* and *Mysis* when larger – 10cm (4in) upwards
SG: 1.020–1.022
Invertebrate compatibility: Yes, when small – 7.5cm (3in)

This species is rarely imported. Despite the unicorn-like growth which gives this species an interesting body shape, its dull colours restrict its popularity. The unicorn tang is at its most attractive when young: it is yellow with dark patches and white spots at 4cm (1½in); and green-yellow with a blue-white belly at 6cm (2½in). As the fish grows it becomes a pale smoke-grey in colour. It tends to eat small aquarium plants. This is a slow-moving fish which looks very graceful in large aquaria.

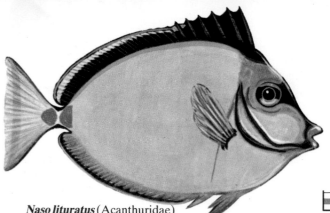

Naso lituratus (Acanthuridae)
Common name: Lipstick tang,
Japanese tang
Origin: Red Sea, East Africa,
Indo-Pacific Ocean
Size: 45cm (18in)
Community tank: Yes, but timid
when small
Food: Algae, *Artemia, Mysis*, dried
food
SG: 1.020–1.022
Invertebrate compatibility: Yes

The lipstick tang is the most attractive
member of its genus. It develops long
extensions to the top and bottom rays
of the tail fin as it grows. This is one of
the most peaceful acanthurids, but it
demands a comparatively large
aquarium or blotchy stress colours
will develop and it may not feed. A
good supply of algae is vital to
maintain the fish in good health. The
colouring improves with age.

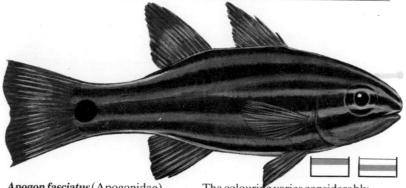

Apogon fasciatus (Apogonidae)
Common name: Striped cardinalfish
Origin: Australasia, Indo-Pacific
Ocean
Size: 13cm (5in)
Community tank: Yes, with
similar-sized fish
Food: *Artemia, Mysis*, chopped fish,
shrimp, earthworms
SG: 1.020–1.024
Invertebrate compatibility: Yes, but
may eat small crustaceans

The colouring varies considerably.
Most commonly they show dark
brown and silver-blue stripes. Rarely
imported, they are best kept in
groups of three or four. Plenty of
hiding places should be provided, as
this fish is shy and retiring. Like
others in the family these are
mouth-brooders, but there are no
reports of the young being
successfully reared. Very much
smaller fish may be eaten,
particularly at night.

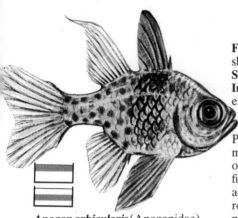

Food: *Artemia, Mysis*, chopped shrimp, shellfish
SG: 1.020–1.022
Invertebrate compatibility: Yes, except with small shrimps

Apogon orbicularis (Apogonidae)
Common name: Pyjama cardinal, Spotted cardinal
Origin: Australasia, Indo-Pacific Ocean
Size: 10cm (4in)
Community tank: Yes, with other peaceful species

Pyjama cardinals are one of the few marine fish which enjoy the company of their own kind. These chunky little fish are easily shocked if carelessly acclimatised, but normally soon recover. This species has a unique pattern among the Apogonidae (the marine cardinalfish, which is not related to the freshwater characin which is also called the cardinal). This species looks most attractive when kept in groups of four or more. They are slow moving, and tend to hover in one spot for long periods.

† *Balistapus undulatus* (Balistidae)
Common name: Undulate trigger
Origin: East Africa, Indo-Pacific Ocean
Size: 30cm (12in)
Community tank: No, keep alone or with other strong, aggressive species
Food: Shrimps, shellfish, chopped fish
SG: 1.020–1.022
Invertebrate compatibility: No, except with some large anemones

This beautiful fish is, unfortunately, one of the most aggressive species of triggerfish. Even when small – 5cm (2in) – it will often harrass and seriously injure much larger fish. It is best kept alone and should only be considered as a community fish where the other inhabitants are larger and equally bad tempered. Like all triggerfish, it has stiff dorsal and anal spines with which it locks itself into its favourite hiding place. These spines can only be forcibly depressed after pressing the second dorsal spine which acts as a releasing trigger.

43

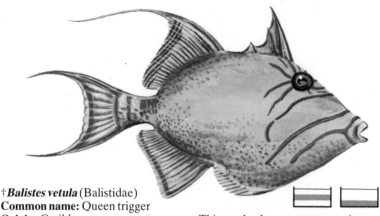

†*Balistes vetula* (Balistidae)
Common name: Queen trigger
Origin: Caribbean
Size: 30cm (12in)
Community tank: Yes, with large, lively fish in large aquaria
Food: Shrimps, shellfish, chopped fish
SG: 1.022–1.025
Invertebrate compatibility: Not compatible

This used to be a common species on the European market but is now rarely available. Temperament varies greatly with individuals, and some can be very aggressive. If kept alone, queen triggers become very tame. It is a very hardy species, and a captive lifespan of five or more years can be expected.

†*Balistoides niger* (Balistidae)
Common name: Clown trigger
Origin: East Africa, Australasia, Indo-Pacific Ocean
Size: 45cm (18in)
Community tank: Yes when small – under 10cm (4in). Keep with lively species
Food: Shrimps, shellfish, chopped fish
SG: 1.020–1.022
Invertebrate compatibility: Only with large anemones

The clown trigger is generally considered the most beautiful member of the family and this is reflected in its high price. Demands good husbandry, but rewards this with hardiness and a long lifespan. The clown trigger should be the last fish introduced into the community tank, as it will often attack newcomers. Large specimens – over 20.5cm (8in) – are best kept alone. Like other triggerfish, the clown trigger will grunt loudly when angry or aroused.

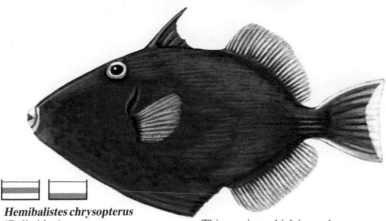

Hemibalistes chrysopterus
(Balistidae)
Common name: Gold-finned trigger
Origin: Indo-Pacific Ocean
Size: 20.5cm (8in)
Community tank: Yes, with medium to large fish
Food: Shrimps, shellfish, chopped fish
SG: 1.020–1.022
Invertebrate compatibility: Only with anemones

This species, which is rarely imported, draws its name from the yellow colour of the pectoral fins. The dorsal and anal fins are pink and the throat is suffused, to a greater or lesser extent, with blue. It is generally more peaceful than *Balistes niger*, but can be aggressive on occasion. One of the more timid Balistidae, this species tends to hide in its own territory for much of the time.

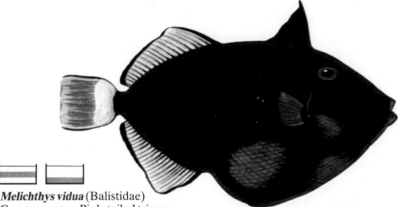

Melichthys vidua (Balistidae)
Common name: Pink-tailed trigger
Origin: Indo-Pacific and Mid-Pacific Oceans
Size: 30cm (12in)
Community tank: Yes, with all but the smallest and most delicate species
Food: Shrimps, shellfish, chopped fish
SG: 1.019–1.022
Invertebrate compatibility: Only with anemones

This is probably the most peaceful species of triggerfish. Provided it has adequate swimming space it will usually not interfere with other species. Although not as hardy as most of the family it deserves greater popularity. Pink-tailed triggers are less prone to digging and moving tank decor than other members of the Balistidae.

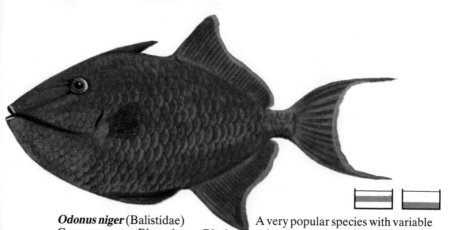

Odonus niger (Balistidae)
Common name: Blue trigger, Black trigger, Green trigger
Origin: Red Sea, Indo-Pacific Ocean
Size: 20.5cm (8in)
Community tank: Yes with similar-sized fish
Food: Shrimps, shellfish, fish
SG: Red Sea origin 1.025–1.030; otherwise 1.020–1.022
Invertebrate compatibility: Only with large anemones

A very popular species with variable colouring, as shown by the range of common names. The opaque anal and dorsal fins allow the attractive swimming movement, unique to the Balistidae and Monacanthidae, to be seen at its best. As the blue trigger grows the bright red incisors give a very malicious appearance. Blue triggers have a reputation for re-arranging the decor and chewing aquarium equipment.

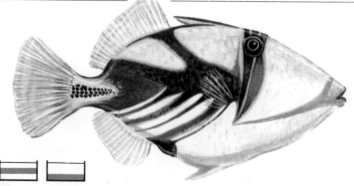

Rhineacanthus aculeatus (Balistidae)
Common name: Picasso trigger, Humu-humu
Origin: Indo-Pacific Ocean
Size: 30cm (12in)
Community tank: Yes, with similar-sized or larger fish which are able to fend for themselves, such as wrasses, groupers, and surgeons
Food: Shrimps, shellfish, chopped fish
SG: 1.019–1.024

Invertebrate compatibility: No

This very common and hardy species is probably the most popular of the Balistidae. It becomes very tame and soon learns to recognise its owner and take food from his or her fingers. This fish has probably the longest common name of any – Humu-humu-nuku-nuku-a-puaa – which translates from Hawaiian to mean 'the fish with a needle and a snout like a pig'.

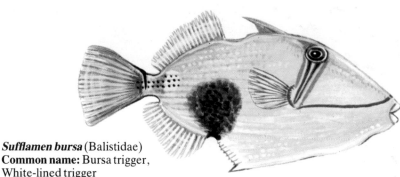

Sufflamen bursa (Balistidae)
Common name: Bursa trigger,
White-lined trigger
Origin: Indo-Pacific Ocean
Size: 20.5cm (8in)
Community tank: Yes, with
similar-sized fish. This is one of the
more peaceful members of the
Balistidae
Food: Shrimps, shellfish, chopped
fish
SG: 1.020–1.022
Invertebrate compatibility: Only with
large anemones such as *Radianthus*
and *Stoicactis* species

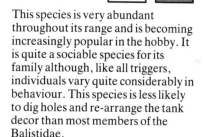

This species is very abundant
throughout its range and is becoming
increasingly popular in the hobby. It
is quite a sociable species for its
family although, like all triggers,
individuals vary quite considerably in
behaviour. This species is less likely
to dig holes and re-arrange the tank
decor than most members of the
Balistidae.

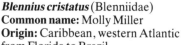

Blennius cristatus (Blenniidae)
Common name: Molly Miller
Origin: Caribbean, western Atlantic
from Florida to Brazil
Size: 10cm (4in)
Community tank: Yes
Food: Shrimps, chopped shellfish,
dried food
SG: 1.020–1.025
Invertebrate compatibility: Yes, but
will eat small crustaceans

This species is occasionally seen
among imports from Florida and is
well worth obtaining. They have
well-developed characters, are very
inquisitive and, if given the
opportunity will climb out of the
aquarium. Tanks must therefore be
well covered to avoid escapes. If a
pair can be found, spawning can be
expected. Eggs are laid on rocks or
shells and guarded by the male, which
is very aggressive towards others of
his sex.

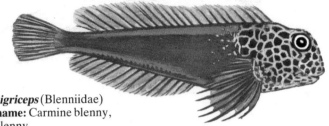

Blennius nigriceps (Blenniidae)
Common name: Carmine blenny,
Cardinal blenny
Origin: Mediterranean coasts of
France, Spain and Italy
Size: 4cm (1½in)
Community tank: Yes, with small,
non-aggressive species
Food: *Artemia, Mysis*, chopped
shellfish, dried food
SG: 1.023–1.026
Invertebrate compatibility: Yes, but
do not keep with large crustaceans,
which are likely to eat the fish

Although not available commercially
in Britain, holidaymakers to the
Mediterranean may be able to catch
their own specimens. This stunning
little fish is very quick to retreat
among rocks, so some patience is
needed. The Blenniidae make
admirable community tank fish and
are very useful scavengers.

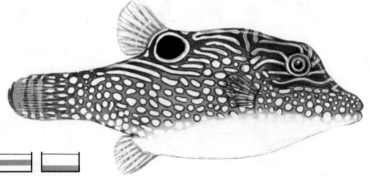

Canthigaster solandri
(Canthigasteridae)
Common name: Margarita puffer,
Sharp nosed puffer
Origin: Red Sea, Indo-Pacific Ocean,
Polynesia
Size: 10cm (4in)
Community tank: Yes, with
non-aggressive species
Food: *Mysis*, shellfish, chopped fish,
shrimps
SG: Red Sea origin 1.025–1.030;
otherwise 1.020–1.022
Invertebrate compatibility: Not
compatible

This is a common species which is
very hardy once settled. It is initially
very nervous and care must be taken
in acclimatising it to new aquaria.
Like others in the family they will
inflate the belly with water when
alarmed, becoming almost spherical.
It is cruel to deliberately try to elicit
this fear response. They perform a
useful job of scavenging in the
fish-only aquarium (as opposed to the
fish and invertebrate aquarium), as
the Canthigasteridae will eat almost
anything edible.

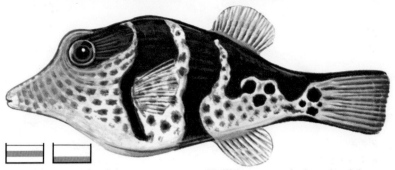

Canthigaster valentini
(Canthigasteridae)
Common name: Valentine puffer
Origin: East Africa, Indo-Pacific
Ocean
Size: 20.5cm (8in)
Community tank: Yes, with
similar-sized fish
Food: Shrimps, shellfish, fish
SG: 1.020–1.022
Invertebrate compatibility: No

Unlike most tropical marine fish
which are happy at temperatures
between 24–26.5 deg C (75–80 deg
F), *C valentini* prefers temperatures
nearer 29 deg C (84 deg F). When
lifted from the water it will inflate the
belly and often croak. This should be
avoided except when necessary as it is
cruel, and the puffer may well bite the
offending hand.

Gnathanodon speciosus (Carangidae)
Common name: Golden caranx,
Barred jack
Origin: Red Sea, Indo-Pacific Ocean
Size: 90cm (36in) plus
Community tank: Yes, when
small – under 10cm – but provide
plenty of swimming space
Food: *Artemia, Mysis* and dried food
when small – 8cm (3in) – any
meat-based food when larger
SG: Red Sea origin 1.025–1.030;
otherwise 1.020–1.022
Invertebrate compatibility: Yes, with
sessile invertebrates. It may eat small
crustaceans, however

The Carangidae are only rarely
available in sizes to suit home
aquaria. They grow very rapidly, but
when young are a beautiful liquid
gold colour, with brown-black
vertical stripes. The illustration
shows the adolescent colouring, the
gold fading to silver. When adult *G.
speciosus* is plain silver with uneven
dark brown spots. An ideal choice for
the large community tank when
small, the golden caranx has a large
mouth and might well eat smaller
tank-mates when larger, however.
The Carangidae all require plenty of
swimming space.

†*Aeoliscus strigatus* (Centriscidae)
Common name: Striped shrimpfish
Origin: Indo-Pacific Ocean
Size: 10cm (4in)
Community tank: No, except with seahorses and pipefish
Food: *Calanus, Artemia* nauplii, *Daphnia, Cyclops*
SG: 1.020–1.022
Invertebrate compatibility: Yes, but do not keep with large crustaceans

This is one of the most peculiar fish in the world. It is laterally compressed to a very high degree and normally swims head-down. These adaptations permit an unusual relationship with long-spined sea-urchins. *A. strigatus* is never found far from sea-urchins and when threatened will hide, head-down, among the spines, where it is almost invisible. Shrimpfish are difficult to transport safely but three or four, together with an urchin, make one of the most interesting exhibits. They are sensitive to copper, and so care must be taken when using copper sulphate based medications. Only the slowest and most peaceful fish may be considered as suitable tank-mates.

Apolemichthys trimaculatus
(Chaetodontidae)
Common name: Flagfin angel, Three spot angel
Origin: Indo-Pacific Ocean
Size: 25cm (10in)
Community tank: Yes, but not with the more competitive species, or they may not get a fair share of the food
Food: *Mysis*, chopped shrimp, shellfish, fish and dried food
SG: 1.020–1.022
Invertebrate compatibility: Yes, when small – under 10cm (4in) – but some larger specimens prove destructive

This attractive species is becoming more readily available, but has not yet gained the popularity of many other marine angelfish species. Specimens under 10cm (4in) are the easiest to acclimatise, but are most often seen larger than this. Occasional large specimens are reluctant to feed, but most will learn to take the commercially available foods provided they do not have to compete with aggressively greedy species. Like most angelfish it is initially shy, but eventually becomes tame and makes a good display fish.

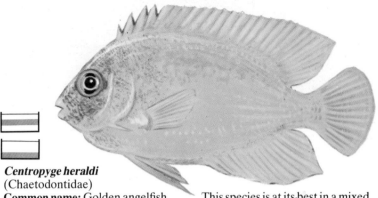

Centropyge heraldi
(Chaetodontidae)
Common name: Golden angelfish,
Lemonpeel angel
Origin: Western Pacific Ocean
Size: 10cm (4in)
Community tank: Yes, but should not
be kept with *C. flavissimus*
Food: *Artemia, Mysis*, chopped
shellfish, dried food, vegetable
matter
SG: 1.020–1.022
Invertebrate compatibility: Yes, but
may damage those creatures with
feathery appendages

This species is at its best in a mixed
fish and invertebrate aquarium where
there is plenty of rock work and a
good growth of algae on which it can
browse throughout the day. Given
these conditions *C. heraldi* is usually
long-lived, and its rich yellow
colouring makes a welcome addition
to most tanks. However, it often fares
badly in the barer confines of the
fish-only aquarium so ensure this
species is feeding well before
purchasing.

Centropyge tibicen (Chaetodontidae)
Common name: Tibicen angel, Black
angel
Origin: Philippines, Melanesia, East
Indies
Size: 13cm (5in)
Community tank: Yes, but can be
very timid and reluctant to compete
Food: *Artemia, Mysis*, dried food,
vegetable matter
SG: 1.020–1.022
Invertebrate compatibility: Yes, but

may damage creatures with feathery
appendages

When in peak condition and in the
right environment this species is very
eye-catching: the yellow edging to
dorsal and anal fins is intense; the
black is rich and velvety; and the
white, a pure enamel. However, all
these colours will fade if the fish is out
of condition. It will also hide, and
may even starve to death, if pestered.

53

Chaetodon auriga (Chaetodontidae)
Common name: Threadfin butterfly
Origin: Indian, western and central
Pacific Oceans
Size: 23cm (9in)
Community tank: Yes, but none of
the butterflies should be kept
in small aquaria
Food: *Artemia*, chopped shrimp,
chopped shellfish occasionally
dried food
SG: 1.020–1.022
Invertebrate compatibility: No,
except with hardy crustaceans such as
hermit crabs

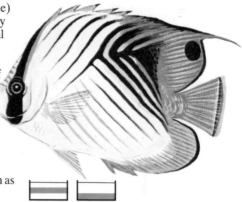

The graceful threadfin butterfly is one
of the hardiest of the butterflyfish, a
family which is generally considered
best left to more advanced aquarists.
All the *Chaetodon* species demand
perfect water conditions but of these,

C. auriga, offers one of the best
chances of long-term success for the
aquarist. The extension of the dorsal
fin, from which the common name
derives, does not develop until the
fish is about 10cm (4in) long.

Chaetodon capistratus
(Chaetodontidae)
Common name: Foureye butterfly
Origin: Caribbean and tropical
Atlantic Ocean
Size: 15cm (6in)
Community tank: Yes, with peaceful
species
Food: *Artemia*, chopped shrimp,
chopped shellfish
SG: 1.022–1.025
Invertebrate compatibility: Like most
Chaetodon species this fish will eat or
injure most of the commonly kept
invertebrates. Only hardy
crustaceans can be safely considered

The foureye butterfly derives its
common name from the eye-spot
near the tail. Such eye-spots are
believed to have evolved to deflect
the attention of predators from the
vulnerable head. Like many species
of *Chaetodon* a black stripe hides the
real eye. Once feeding
enthusiastically they are quite hardy
but some specimens will starve rather
than take commercially available
foods.

54

Chaetodon citrinellus

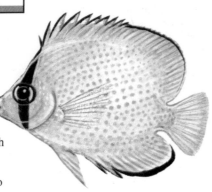

(Chaetodontidae)
Common name: Lemon butterfly,
Citron butterfly, Speckled butterfly
Origin: Indian and Pacific Oceans
Size: 13cm (5in)
Community tank: Yes, a peaceful if
rather delicate species
Food: *Artemia*, chopped shellfish
SG: 1.020–1.022
Invertebrate compatibility: Only with
hardy crustaceans

The lemon butterfly usually proves to
be more shy than many *Chaetodon*
species. It frequently refuses to feed,
but will sometimes be tempted by live
Artemia or coral. Great care should
be taken to purchase only those seen
to feed readily. Although not the
brightest *Chaetodon* this species is
usually inexpensive.

Chaetodon collaris (Chaetodontidae)
Common name: Pakistan butterfly
Origin: Central Indian Ocean; very
common around Sri Lanka
Size: 15cm (6in)
Community tank: Yes, with similarly
peaceful fish
Food: *Artemia, Mysis*, chopped
shrimp, chopped shellfish, very
occasionally dried food
SG: 1.020–1.022
Invertebrate compatibility: Only
hardy crustaceans can be considered

The rich chocolate brown body
colour of the Pakistan butterfly is
unique among butterflyfish. This and
its comparative ease of maintenance,
when compared with many
chaetodons, has made it one of the
most popular of its genus. Provided
good water conditions and plenty of
swimming space is provided they
usually quickly overcome any initial
shyness and learn to compete for
food. Small specimens, around 8cm
(3in), are usually the easiest to
acclimatise.

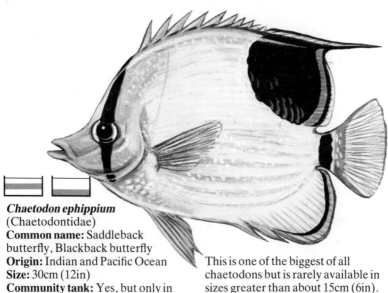

Chaetodon ephippium
(Chaetodontidae)
Common name: Saddleback
butterfly, Blackback butterfly
Origin: Indian and Pacific Ocean
Size: 30cm (12in)
Community tank: Yes, but only in
large aquaria
Food: *Artemia*, chopped shrimp,
chopped shellfish
SG: 1.020–1.022
Invertebrate compatibility: No

This is one of the biggest of all
chaetodons but is rarely available in
sizes greater than about 15cm (6in).
Large specimens are often reluctant
to feed, but smaller specimens can
usually be tempted by live *Artemia*.
In good health this is one of the most
attractive butterflyfish.

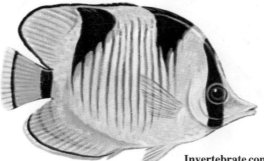

Chaetodon falcula (Chaetodontidae)
Common name: Black wedge
butterfly
Origin: Red Sea, Indian and western
Pacific Oceans
Size: 20.5cm (8in)
Community tank: Yes, with peaceful
species
Food: *Artemia, Mysis*, chopped
shrimp, chopped shellfish,
occasionally dried food
SG: Red Sea origin 1.025–1.030;
otherwise 1.020–1.022

Invertebrate compatibility: No, very
small specimens are quite peaceful,
but those over 6cm (2½in) can be
very destructive

This beautiful species is well worth
searching for. Although it is not
imported as frequently as many
members of its genus it is justifiably
popular. It rarely presents feeding
problems and will usually compete
more actively for food than most
species. When at its best the
yellowish areas of the body are a rich
glowing orange.

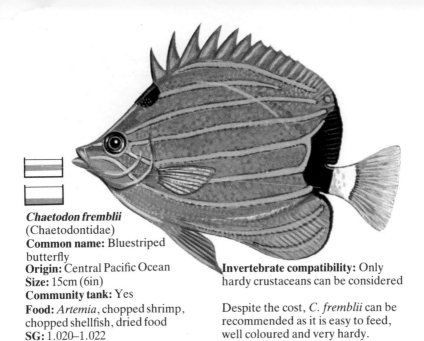

Chaetodon fremblii
(Chaetodontidae)
Common name: Bluestriped
butterfly
Origin: Central Pacific Ocean
Size: 15cm (6in)
Community tank: Yes
Food: *Artemia*, chopped shrimp,
chopped shellfish, dried food
SG: 1.020–1.022

Invertebrate compatibility: Only
hardy crustaceans can be considered

Despite the cost, *C. fremblii* can be
recommended as it is easy to feed,
well coloured and very hardy.

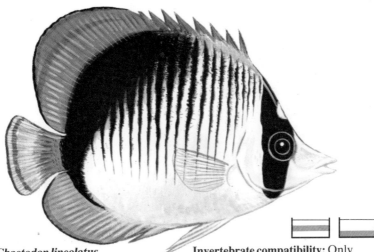

Chaetodon lineolatus
(Chaetodontidae)
Common name: Lined butterfly
Origin: Indian and Pacific Oceans
Size: 30cm (12in)
Community tank: Yes, small
specimens – under 8cm (3in) – are
ideal
Food: *Artemia*, chopped shrimp,
chopped shellfish, dried food
SG: 1.020–1.022

Invertebrate compatibility: Only
hardy crustaceans can be considered

This is one of the largest *Chaetodon*
species but it is only rarely seen larger
than 15cm (6in) and at this and
smaller sizes it makes an ideal
aquarium fish. Unlike many
butterflyfish it feeds readily and will
compete with more lively fish to
obtain its share.

Chaetodon lunula (Chaetodontidae)
Common name: Moon butterfly,
Red-striped butterfly
Origin: Indian and Pacific Oceans
Size: 20.5cm (8in)
Community tank: Yes, with
smaller and peaceful species
Food: *Artemia, Mysis,*
chopped shrimp,
chopped shellfish,
occasionally dried food
SG: 1.020–1.022

Invertebrate compatibility: This is
one of the most persistently
destructive butterflyfish; only large
crustaceans are safe

The moon butterfly is one of few in
the genus which can safely be
recommended for the beginner. Best
purchased at about 8cm (3in) this
richly coloured fish usually proves
very hardy. Reluctant feeders can
usually be tempted with live *Artemia*.
Once it begins feeding it will quickly
learn to accept almost any offering,
even when fed from the fingers.

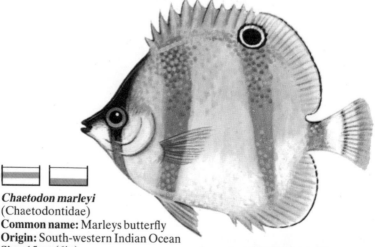

Chaetodon marleyi
(Chaetodontidae)
Common name: Marleys butterfly
Origin: South-western Indian Ocean
Size: 15cm (6in)
Community tank: Yes, with
similar-sized or smaller fish
Food: *Artemia*, shrimps, chopped
shellfish
SG: 1.020–1.022
Invertebrate compatibility: Only
hardy crustaceans can be considered

A rarely available fish in Europe or
the United States since few fish are
ever imported from South Africa.
The colour varies with age; the young
are yellow with orange vertical bands
which become darker with age.
Whatever the age *C. marleyi* displays
a distinct eye-spot.

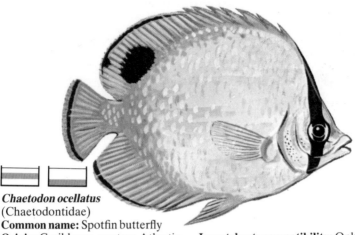

Chaetodon ocellatus
(Chaetodontidae)
Common name: Spotfin butterfly
Origin: Caribbean, western Atlantic
Size: 20.5cm (8in)
Community tank: Yes, with small peaceful species
Food: *Artemia*, chopped shrimp, chopped shellfish, vegetable matter
SG: 1.022–1.025

Invertebrate compatibility: Only with hardy crustaceans

Less often seen in Europe than in America, *C. ocellatus* is frequently difficult to feed. It is quietly elegant, however.

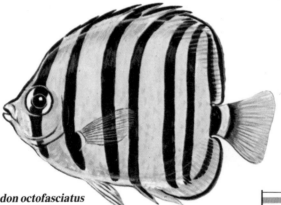

Chaetodon octofasciatus
(Chaetodontidae)
Common name: Eight-banded butterfly
Origin: Indo-Pacific Ocean
Size: 15cm (6in)
Community tank: Yes, but occasional specimens can be surprisingly aggressive, particularly towards other chaetodons
Food: *Artemia, Mysis*, chopped shellfish, chopped fish, algae
Invertebrate compatibility: No, particularly destructive towards feather-duster worms.

This species is one of many perplexing butterflyfish; some specimens refuse to feed and starve to death, while others prove to be gluttons and go on to live happily for several years. Specimens between 5–8cm (2–3in) are usually the easiest to acclimatise, larger specimens being set in their habits, and younger fish requiring a near continual supply of food if they are to prosper. The attractive colouring makes this an instantly appealing fish, nevertheless.

Chaetodon ornatissimus
(Chaetodontidae)
Common name: Ornate butterfly
Origin: Western and central
Pacific Ocean
Size: 15cm (6in)
Community tank: Yes,
with placid species
Food: Live coral, *Tubifex*,
live shellfish
SG: 1.020–1.022
Invertebrate compatibility: Often
destructive to all invertebrates
except crustaceans

This extremely attractive species is
one of the most difficult butterflyfish
to maintain for any length of time. In
the wild it feeds on live corals and
little else. This diet is very difficult
and expensive to reproduce in
captivity and only very rarely will it
adapt to other, more readily available
foods. Occasional specimens will
take live *Tubifex* or live shellfish.

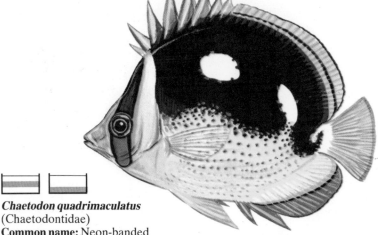

Chaetodon quadrimaculatus
(Chaetodontidae)
Common name: Neon-banded
butterfly
Origin: Indo-Pacific and central
Pacific Oceans
Size: 15cm (6in)
Community tank: Yes, with
similar-sized, peaceful species
Food: Live coral, *Artemia*, *Tubifex*,
live shellfish
SG: 1.020–1.022
Invertebrate compatibility: Only with
crustaceans

This outstandingly coloured
Chaetodon is one which needs to be
selected with some care. Many will
quickly learn to take commercially
available foods but others are very
reluctant feeders. Reluctant feeders
can sometimes be encouraged to feed
by introducing invertebrates into the
aquarium since these offer the fish
something to peck at and so stimulate
the appetite.

Chaetodon speculum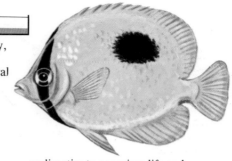
(Chaetodontidae)
Common name: One-spot butterfly,
Tear-drop butterfly
Origin: Indo-Pacific Oceans, central
Pacific Ocean
Size: 13cm (5in)
Community tank: Yes, with
similar-sized or smaller species
Food: *Artemia*, chopped shrimp,
chopped shellfish
SG: 1.020–1.022
Invertebrate compatibility: Only
hardy crustaceans can be considered

When in good health this fish displays
a rich golden yellow colour which
makes it a very attractive addition to
the community tank. Specimens
around 6cm (2½in) are the easiest to

acclimatise to aquarium life and,
after initial feeding with live *Artemia*,
generally learn to take other foods.
Very small specimens, around 2.5cm
(1in), are often available but should
be avoided except by experienced
hobbyists. These, like all very small
chaetodons, need an almost constant
supply of food if they are to develop.

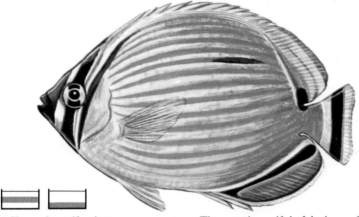

† **Chaetodon trifasciatus**
(Chaetodontidae)
Common name: Rainbow butterfly,
Redfin butterfly
Origin: Indian, western and central
Pacific Ocean
Size: 15cm (6in)
Community tank: No, a delicate
species to be kept with only the most
placid fish
Food: Live coral, *Tubifex*, *Artemia*,
live shellfish
SG: 1.020–1.022
Invertebrate compatibility: Yes, but
not with live corals

The most beautiful of the butterflies,
the rainbow butterfly qualifies as one
of the few *Chaetodon* species suitable
for the invertebrate tank solely
because the large majority of
specimens will not eat at all in
captivity. The range of foods above
indicates those which may be tried
with some hope of success, not a
selection which generally proves
acceptable. A similar species from
the Red Sea, *C. austriacus*, is
somewhat easier to acclimatise but is
only very rarely available and much
more expensive.

61

Chaetodon vagabundus
(Chaetodontidae)

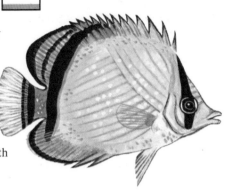

Common name: Vagabond butterfly
Origin: Indian and Pacific Oceans
Size: 17cm (7in)
Community tank: Yes, one of the best *Chaetodon* species for a mixed tank
Food: *Artemia*, chopped shrimp, chopped shellfish, dried food
SG: 1.020–1.022
Invertebrate compatibility: Only with larger crustaceans

The vagabond butterfly is the ideal first *Chaetodon* as it is hardy, feeds well, is inexpensive and, while not aggressive, will stand up for itself.

Although not as gaudy as some of its genus *C. vagabundus* is an elegant fish and justifiably popular.

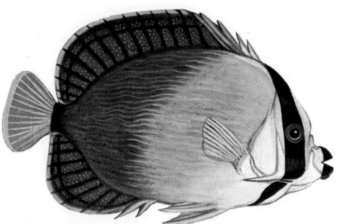

decorative algae, although occasional specimens are destructive

Chaetodontoplus mesoleucus
(Chaetodontidae)
Common name: Orange-tail angel, Yellow-tail angel, Butterfly angel
Origin: Indo-Pacific Ocean, Australasia
Size: 15cm (6in)
Community tank: Yes, with similar-sized, peaceful species
Food: *Artemia, Tubifex*, live shellfish, algae
SG: 1.020–1.022
Invertebrate compatibility: Yes, generally well behaved, eating only

This species is an angelfish, as defined by the sharp spines on the gill-plate, but it looks and behaves like a butterflyfish. The subdued and elegant colouring makes a pleasant contrast to some of the more gaudy species. Frequently a very reluctant feeder, often only the stimulus of being in an invertebrate aquarium – with the varied menu that provides – persuading it to eat at all. The genus *Chaetodontoplus* is not recommended for beginners.

Heniochus varius (Chaetodontidae)
Common name: Brown wimplefish,
Humphead bannerfish
Origin: Indo-Pacific Ocean,
Australasia
Size: 20.5cm (8in)
Community tank: Yes, with small
peaceful species
Food: *Artemia, Mysis*, chopped
shellfish, vegetable matter
SG: 1.020–1.022
Invertebrate compatibility: Only
hardy crustaceans can be safely
considered

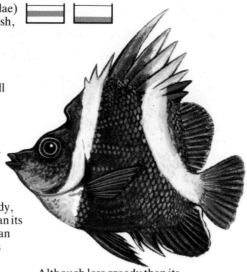

The brown wimplefish is less hardy,
less common and less popular than its
relative, *H. acuminatus*, but it is an
interesting fish, particularly in its
larger sizes. When young it has a
similar body shape to other
Heniochus species, but as it grows the
hump, from which the alternative
common name is derived, develops
until when adult it appears a sizeable
bite has been taken from the head.

Although less greedy than its
common relative, specimens of *H.
varius* of about 8cm (3in) can usually
be tempted with live *Artemia*. Once
their fast is broken they generally
acclimatise quite quickly.

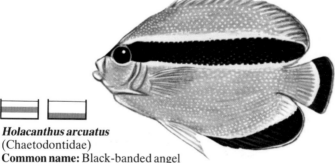

Holacanthus arcuatus
(Chaetodontidae)
Common name: Black-banded angel
Origin: Hawaii
Size: 20.5cm (8in)
Community tank: Yes, with
similar-sized, peaceful species
Food: Algae, *Artemia*, chopped
shellfish
SG: 1.020–1.022
Invertebrate compatibility: Variable;
some specimens are quite well
behaved but many larger ones are
destructive

This species is common throughout
its limited range but is infrequently
available to the hobbyist. It is an
elegant fish which displays itself well
in large tanks. It is often difficult to
persuade it to eat, however. Small
specimens are easier to acclimatise to
the aquarium but these are rarely
seen, most being offered for sale at
around 15cm (6in).

65

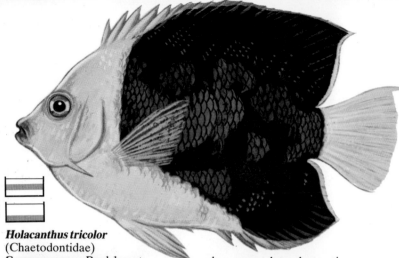

Holacanthus tricolor
(Chaetodontidae)
Common name: Rock beauty
Origin: Caribbean, tropical western Atlantic
Size: 30cm (12in)
Community tank: yes, but large specimens sometimes become aggressive, particularly towards other Chaetodontidae
Food: Algae, *Artemia*, shrimps, chopped shellfish and fish, dried food
SG: 1.022–1.025
Invertebrate compatibility: Yes, when young, later destructive

This eye-catching fish stands out in any collection. The elegant trailing extensions to the dorsal and anal fins develop with age. Small specimens are particularly attractive having much less black in the body than the adult, which is shown in the illustration. Youngsters are more adaptable to the commercially available foods.

Parachaetodon ocellatus
(Chaetodontidae)
Common name: Ocellate butterfly
Origin: Indo-Pacific Ocean
Size: 15cm (6in)
Community tank: Yes, with similarly peaceful fish
Food: *Artemia, Mysis*, chopped shrimp, chopped shellfish
SG: 1.020–1.022
Invertebrate compatibility: No; not as destructive as many of the butterflyfish but still not to be trusted

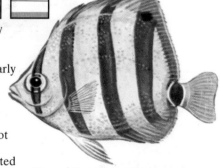

P. ocellatus is an elegant fish which fares best in the company of its own kind. Provided it is given three or four heavy feeds with live adult *Artemia* it generally settles quickly in the aquarium and from then on accepts other foods. If this initial live food is omitted it frequently starves.

The ocellate butterfly sports two eye-spots, one at the root of the tail and the other in the soft part of the dorsal fin, but both fade somewhat with age. This species, like most butterflyfish, demands ideal water conditions and, particularly when small, cannot be recommended for the beginner.

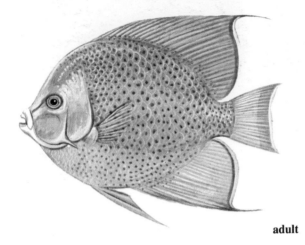

adult

juvenile

Pomacanthus arcuatus
(Chaetodontidae)
Common name: Black angel, Grey
angel
Origin: Caribbean, western Atlantic
Size: 60cm (24in)
Community tank: Yes, when
small – under 13cm (5in) – but large
specimens are often very aggressive
Food: Algae, chopped shrimp,
chopped shellfish, dried food
SG: 1.022–1.025
Invertebrate compatibility: Yes, but
only when very young; even small
species will damage delicately
structured invertebrates

All the *Pomacanthus* species show a
radical change of colouring as they
mature. When young this species is
black with yellow stripes, and has
blue tips to the pelvic and anal fins.
As it grows the yellow and blue fade
to leave a dull grey adult. It rarely
grows to more than 30cm (12in) in
captivity. Black angels and their close
relations, *P. paru*, are now being
bred in captivity but this is not a
proposition for the home aquarist.
All the *Pomacanthus* species are avid
algae eaters so the decorative species
should be excluded.

adult

juvenile

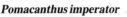

Pomacanthus imperator
(Chaetodontidae)
Common name: Emperor angel
Origin: Red Sea, Indian Ocean,
western and central Pacific Ocean
(except Hawaii)
Size: 38cm (15in)
Community tank: Yes, but should not
be kept with other *Pomacanthus*
species or serious fighting may result
Food: Algae, *Mysis*, chopped shrimp,
chopped shellfish, dried food
SG: Red Sea origin 1.025–1.030;
otherwise 1.020–1.022
Invertebrate compatibility: Varies
considerably from specimen to
specimen. Some are very destructive,
particularly when large, but most are
safe with the less-delicate
invertebrates

The emperor angel is one of the most
stunningly coloured marine fish and is
justifiably popular despite its high
price. The young display a pattern of
concentric circles of blue and white,
but by the time it has grown to about
10cm (4in) this fades and the adult
colour pattern begins to develop.
This fish demands plenty of room and
ideal water conditions. Closely
related species *P. annularis* and *P.
semicirculatus* show similar juvenile
patterns but in *P. annularis* the
striping is nearly vertical and the tail
clear, while in *P. semicirculatus* the
juvenile shows semicircular banding.

68

Pomacanthus paru (Chaetodontidae)
Common name: French angel
Origin: Caribbean and tropical
Atlantic Ocean
Size: 40cm (16in)
Community tank: Yes, when
small – under 15cm (6in) – but large
specimens are often very aggressive,
particularly towards other
Chaetodontidae
Food: Algae, *Mysis*, chopped
shrimps, shellfish, dried food
Invertebrate compatibility: Yes, but
only when small. Large specimens
are destructive and in the wild
regularly eat sponge, which they can
be expected to repeat in captivity

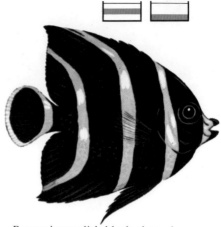

This is probably one of the two most
popular of all Caribbean species. The
illustration shows a juvenile. Very
similar to the juvenile black angel,
the black area in the tail of the French
angel is more circular. When mature,

P. paru is purplish-black, the scales
edged with yellow, and there is a
yellow ring around the eye. This is
one of the easiest of the large angels
to maintain, and can be expected to
live a long time – seven or eight years
being quite common.

Pomacanthus semicirculatus
(Chaetodontidae)
Common name: Koran angel
Origin: Red Sea, Indian and western
Pacific Oceans
Size: 45cm (18in)
Community tank: Yes, when
small – 15cm (6in) – but large
specimens can be aggressive,
particularly towards other
chaetodons
Food: Almost anything edible and of
a suitable size. A high proportion of
vegetable matter should be included.
SG: 1.020–1.025
Invertebrate compatibility: Only
large anemones and large crustaceans
can be expected to remain in
reasonable condition

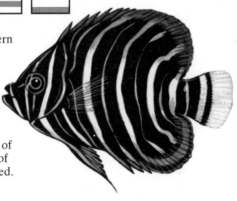

The Koran angel is the most common
Pomacanthus species. This results in
an inexpensive fish, which when
combined with its comparative
hardiness make it the ideal subject for
the beginner contemplating keeping

a marine angelfish. Koran angels can
normally be expected to survive for
several years. When adult the fish is
olive-green, edged with blue and with
blue scribble markings in the tail. It is
from these tail patterns the common
name is derived – legend having it
that Arabian fishermen could discern
quotations from the Koran in these
markings.

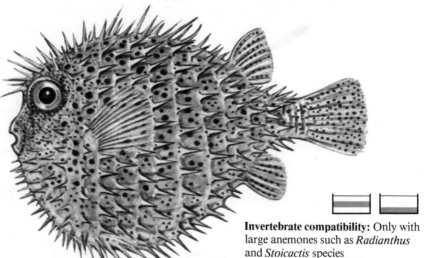

Pygoplites diacanthus
(Chaetodontidae)
Common name: Regal
angel, Royal
empress angel
Origin: Red Sea,
Indo-Pacific
Size: 30cm (12in)
Community tank: Yes,
but only with smaller,
placid species
Food: Chopped shrimp,
chopped shellfish, occasionally
dried food
SG: Red Sea origin 1.025–1.030;
otherwise 1.020–1.022
Invertebrate compatibility: Yes; most
specimens are well behaved except
with molluscs and small crustaceans

There appear to be two races; regal
angels from the Red Sea and the
Maldive Islands are much more
intensely coloured and more ready
feeders than those from the
Philippines.

Invertebrate compatibility: Only with
large anemones such as *Radianthus*
and *Stoicactis* species

Diodon histrix (Diodontidae)
Common name: Porcupine puffer
Origin: Circumtropical
Size: 30cm (12in)
Community tank: Yes, with placid,
similar-sized fish
Food: Chopped shellfish, chopped
fish, worms, shrimp
SG: Red Sea origin 1.025–1.030;
otherwise 1.020–1.022

This species is one of the real
characters among fish. It becomes
ridiculously tame — many specimens
appearing to enjoy gentle
tickling — lives a long time and is
sufficiently hardy to resist the
mistakes of beginners in the hobby.
When alarmed, the fish inflates itself
with water and the sharp spines
radiate out from the body.

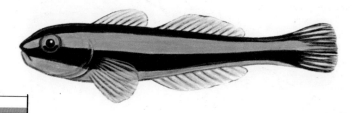

Gobiosoma oceanops (Gobiidae)
Common name: Neon goby
Origin: Caribbean, Florida
Size: 8cm (3in)
Community tank: Yes, with small peaceful species
Food: *Artemia*, zooplankton, chopped shellfish, dried food
SG: 1.022–1.025
Invertebrate compatibility: Yes, an ideal species to add movement to an invertebrate aquarium

This beautiful little fish is justifiably one of the most popular of the smaller Caribbean species. It is ideal for hobbyists with small aquaria. They will sometimes pick parasites from other tank inhabitants. Neon gobies have often bred in captivity. Eggs are usually laid in seashells, both parents guarding the eggs until hatching about ten to twelve days later. The parents will eat newly hatched fry, however. For the first five days the young absorb the yolk-sac but then should be offered *Euplotes* or similar organisms until they are big enough to take *Artemia* nauplii (usually at about a month old).

Lythrypnus dalli (Gobiidae)
Common name: Catalina goby
Origin: Catalina Island, California
Size: 4cm (1½in)
Community tank: No, only with very small, peaceful species
Food: *Artemia*, zooplankton, very finely chopped shellfish, dried food
SG: 1.020–1.022
Invertebrate compatibility: Yes, but do not keep with large crustaceans which may capture and kill them

This beautiful species is one of the jewels among marine fish. Unfortunately it is now only rarely available. It is peaceful towards other species but vigorously defends its territory against its own kind. For this reason, unless pairs can be obtained, they should be kept singly or in sizeable groups. The Gobiidae are characterised by having the pectoral fins modified, to a greater or lesser extent, to form a sucker which is used to help them climb wet rocks and to hold their position against water currents.

71

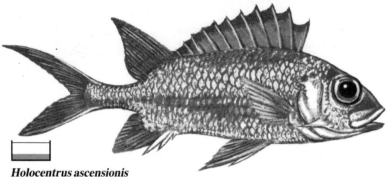

Holocentrus ascensionis
(Holocentridae)
Common name: Longjaw squirrelfish
Origin: Western Atlantic from New York to Brazil
Size: 30cm (12in)
Community tank: Yes, with similar-sized fish
Food: Shrimps, chopped fish
SG: 1.020–1.022
Invertebrate compatibility: Yes, but will eat small crustaceans

All the Holocentridae are nocturnal and cave dwellers. Their tanks should be dimly lit and provided with plenty of rockwork otherwise they prove very shy. As they are one of the few inexpensive red marinefish, apart from Amphiprion species, they merit this extra consideration. Looking their best in groups of five or six, remember they have large mouths and will eat small fish.

Myripristis murdjan (Holocentridae)
Common name: Bigeye squirrelfish
Origin: Indo-Pacific Ocean
Size: 20.5cm (8in)
Community tank: Yes, with similar-sized fish
Food: Shrimps, chopped fish
SG: 1.020–1.022
Invertebrate compatibility: Yes, but will eat small crustaceans

This is one of the reddest fish available to the marine hobbyist and under the correct, low-intensity lighting, it almost glows. The huge, disproportionate eye, characteristic of nocturnal fish, gives the fish an eerie expression but a small group looks very attractive in the lower layers of the aquarium. *M. murdjan* cannot be trusted with small fish, but any which are too big to be swallowed will be ignored.

Bodianus axillaris (Labridae)
Common name: Coral hog fish
Origin: Indo-Pacific Ocean
Size: 20.5cm (8in)
Community tank: Yes, with similar-sized, lively competitive species
Food: Chopped shrimp, chopped shellfish, chopped fish, dried food
SG: 1.020–1.022
Invertebrate compatibility: No, except when very young – under 5cm (2in). Larger specimens are destructive towards all except large anemones and crustaceans

This species has two different colour forms, depending on the sex and age of the fish. Juveniles and females look as the illustration shows. In males the anterior half of the body is purplish brown and the posterior half is rich orange with a black line dividing the two. To obtain a male/female pair it would be necessary to buy two juveniles and rear them together. The dominant fish would become a functional male and the other the female. They have not been bred in captivity but spawning might be a possibility in a very large tank. Either sex is very attractive and as this fish is very hardy it is justifiably popular.

Bodianus rufus (Labridae)
Common name: Spanish hog fish
Origin: Caribbean and Gulf of Mexico
Size: 60cm (24in)
Community tank: Yes, with boisterous competitive species
Food: Shrimps, chopped shellfish, chopped fish, some dried food
SG: 1.022–1.025
Invertebrate compatibility: No. Reasonably well behaved when very young but increasingly destructive with age

This species is very popular both in the United States and in Europe. When small – under 5cm (2in) – it will act as a cleaner, picking parasites from other fish. This habit is lost with age, its diet then encompassing almost anything edible. Although it grows very large in the wild it rarely exceeds 20.5cm (8in) in captivity unless housed in exceptionally large aquaria. The purple-blue and yellow colouring is very striking, and it is among the hardiest of the Labridae.

73

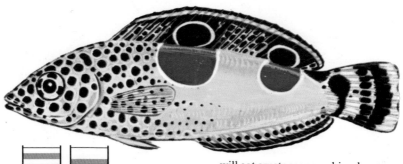

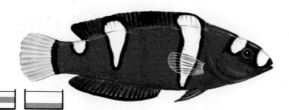

Coris angulata (Labridae)
Common name: Twinspot wrasse
Origin: Red Sea, Indian Ocean
Size: 90cm (36in)
Community tank: Yes, when small – under 15cm (6in) – but increasingly aggressive with age
Food: *Artemia*, chopped shrimp, chopped shellfish, dried food
SG: Red Sea origin 1.025–1.030; otherwise 1.020–1.022
Invertebrate compatibility: Yes, when young, but larger specimens will eat crustaceans, echinoderms and feather-duster worms

This is one of the most sought-after wrasses, for it is an outstanding lower water fish, particularly when young. The illustration shows a juvenile; in life the intensity of the two red dorsal spots is even more pronounced. As the fish ages the red fades and the pure white becomes a dusky grey. Mature adults, which are only ever seen in public aquaria, are uniformly dark.

Coris formosa (Labridae)
Common name: Clown wrasse
Origin: Indian Ocean
Size: 38cm (15in)
Community tank: Yes, a very well-behaved species when kept with similar-sized fish
Food: *Artemia*, chopped shrimp, chopped shellfish, dried food
SG: 1.020–1.022
Invertebrate compatibility: Yes, when small – under 8cm (3in) – but large specimens will eat crustaceans and damage echinoderms and sabellid worms

This species changes colour quite dramatically as it ages but at all stages it is a very beautiful fish. The illustration shows a juvenile. When about 8cm (3in) long the body darkens to almost black. As maturity is reached the body becomes reddish brown with black spots. The fins are edged with blue and there are vivid blue markings around the eye. Like other *Coris* species, this one will dive into the gravel when disturbed and usually spends the night there.

Coris gaimard (Labridae)
Common name: Clown wrasse
Origin: Indo-Pacific and central
Pacific Oceans
Size: 38cm (15in)
Community tank: Yes, one of the
best wrasses for a mixed tank
Food: _Artemia_, chopped shrimp,
chopped shellfish, dried food
SG: 1.020–1.022
Invertebrate compatibility: Yes,
when small – under 8cm (3in) – but
large specimens will eat crustaceans
and damage echinoderms and
sabellid worms

This species is often confused with _C._
formosa, particularly when juvenile,
but _C. formosa_ can be distinguished
by the black spot in the dorsal fin.
When large, _C. gaimard_ retains more
red in the body and is generally
considered the more attractive of the
two species, despite being slightly
more delicate. When first introduced
to the aquarium _C. gaimard_ will often
spend several days beneath the
gravel. As juveniles they will eat
parasites from the skin and fins of
their tank-mates.

Coris julis (Labridae)
Common name: Mediterranean
wrasse
Origin: Mediterranean Sea
Size: 20.5cm (8in)
Community tank: Yes, with lively fish
Food: _Artemia_, chopped shrimp,
chopped shellfish, dried food
Temperature: 16–24 deg C (60–75
deg F)
SG: 1.023–1.026
Invertebrate compatibility: Only safe
with large anemones and crustaceans

This is the only _Coris_ species found
outside the tropics. Although not
available commercially they are very
common in the Mediterranean and
many hobbyists successfully bring
them home at the end of their
holidays. They prefer slightly lower
temperatures than most tropical
marines but will usually adjust to
higher temperatures quite readily.
Large specimens are inclined to be
aggressive but small ones make
welcome additions when kept with
equally boisterous species.

75

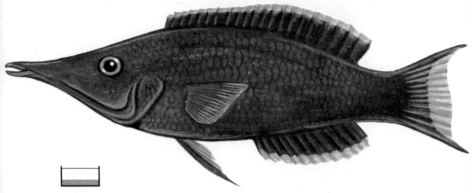

†***Gomphosus coeruleus*** (Labridae)
Common name: Birdnose wrasse
Origin: Indian, western and central
Pacific Ocean
Size: 30cm (12in)
Community tank: No, a very lively
fish best kept with equally
fast-moving species
Food: Shrimp, shellfish, chopped fish
SG: 1.020–1.022
Invertebrate compatibility: Will eat

crustaceans and may damage
echinoderms and sabellid worms

The birdnose wrasse is one of those
species in which the dominant
members become functional males.
These specimens are a uniquely
intense blue-green. Juveniles and
females are brown. This is a very
hardy species of the lower layers, but
it requires plenty of swimming room.

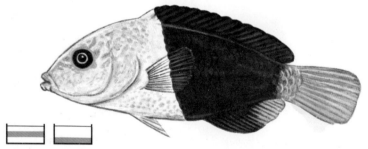

Hemigymnus melapterus (Labridae)
Common name: Half and half wrasse,
Apartheid wrasse
Origin: Indo-Pacific Ocean
Size: 30cm (12in)
Community tank: Yes when
small – under 8cm (3in) – with
peaceful species
Food: *Mysis*, chopped shrimp,
chopped shellfish, vegetable matter
SG: 1.020–1.022
Invertebrate compatibility: No; will
nibble and cause minor damage to
many types of invertebrates

Regularly imported, the half and half
wrasse is slightly more difficult to
maintain than many other Labridae.
Although they feed well they often
slowly loose weight and become
emaciated. Very frequent light
feedings are required, or an
environment from which they can
continually find food. They are quite
attractive when young but become
dull brown with age.

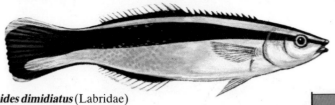

Labroides dimidiatus (Labridae)
Common name: Cleaner wrasse
Origin: Indian and western Pacific
Oceans
Size: 10cm (4in)
Community tank: Yes, but not with
slow-moving species
Food: *Artemia, Mysis*, finely chopped
shellfish, occasionally dried food
SG: 1.020–1.022
Invertebrate compatibility: Yes, but
will peck at delicately structured
invertebrates

This very attractive and common
species performs a very important
task. It picks parasites from fish.
They are so efficient and welcomed
that they are allowed to swim into
the mouths of large fish and clean the
gills. Cleaner wrasse will sometimes
pester individual fish until they are
so distressed they stop feeding. *L.
dimidiatus* should thus not be housed
with *Diodon*, boxfish or puffers.

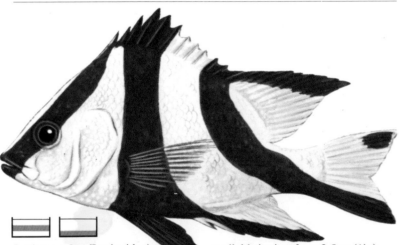

Lutjanus sebae (Lutjanidae)
Common name: Emperor snapper,
Red emperor
Origin: Indian Ocean, Australasia,
western Pacific Ocean
Size: 90cm (36in)
Community tank: Yes, when
small – under 15cm (6in) – and kept
with lively fish
Food: Shrimps, chopped shellfish,
chopped fish
SG: 1.020–1.022
Invertebrate compatibility: Yes, but
will eat crustaceans

This attractive species is often

available in sizes from 2.5cm (1in)
and upwards but it is one of the
fastest-growing fish and will soon
outgrow all but the largest aquarium.
Although reaching 90cm (36in) in the
wild they rarely exceed 25cm (10in) in
captivity. Despite this their
interesting swimming motion,
friendliness, hardiness and bright
colours ensure their popularity.
Emperor snappers have large
mouths, hence the name, and will eat
almost anything. When small, *L.
sebae* can be kept in groups of four or
five, although bullying occurs as they
grow.

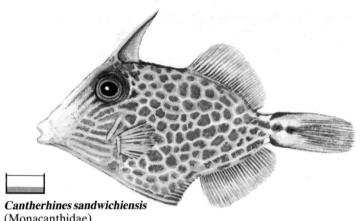

Cantherhines sandwichiensis
(Monacanthidae)
Common name: Common filefish,
Sandwich trigger
Origin: Circumtropical
Size: 38cm (15in)
Community tank: Yes, when
small – under 10cm (4in) – but not
with small wrasses (Labridae)
Food: Chopped shrimp, chopped
shellfish, chopped fish
SG: 1.020–1.025
Invertebrate compatibility: Not
compatible

This family is very closely related to
the Balistidae but the filefish are very
different from the triggers in
behaviour. They are usually peaceful
and occasionally shy. This species is
one of the easiest of the
Monacanthidae for the amateur
aquarist. *C. sandwichiensis* may peck
at the fins of slow-moving species or
those which rest on gravel or among
rocks at night, however.

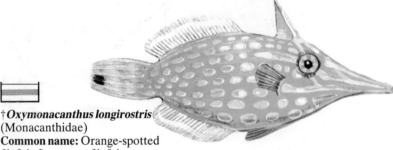

†*Oxymonacanthus longirostris*
(Monacanthidae)
Common name: Orange-spotted
filefish, Longnose filefish
Origin: Indo-Pacific Ocean
Size: 10cm (4in)
Community tank: No, keep only with
very quiet species such as seahorses,
pipefish, small gobies, etc.
Food: Live coral, live *Artemia*, live
bloodworm
SG: 1.020–1.022
Invertebrate compatibility: Yes,
except corals with small polyps

This species is the 'odd man out' in its
family, being totally peaceful,
beautifully coloured and difficult to
feed. The best chance for success is to
keep three or four together in a
heavily furnished tank. Like its
relatives it will erect the rigid dorsal
and anal spines and wedge itself
tightly among coral branches when
frightened or resting.

Monodactylus argenteus
(Monodactylidae)
Common name: Mono, Malayan
angel, Moonfish, Sea kite
Origin: Indo-Pacific Ocean
Size: 23cm (9in)
Community tank: Yes
Food: _Artemia_, shrimps, chopped
fish, dried foods
SG: 1.005–1.022
Invertebrate compatibility: Yes,
but will damage finely structured
invertebrates such as feather-duster
worms

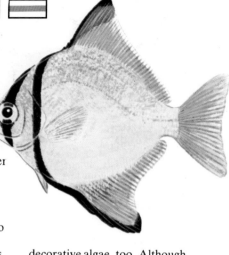

This is one of the few species
available to the aquarist that will
tolerate mildly brackish water up to
full salinity sea-water. As can be
guessed, this is a very hardy species
ideally suited to the beginner. It will
eat almost anything offered and care
must be taken to ensure other
occupants get a fair share of the food.
A certain amount of vegetable matter
is important in its diet; it will eat
decorative algae, too. Although
growing quite large malayan angels
are usually quite peaceful. A similar,
but more vertically elongated species
from west Africa, _M. sebae_, is
sometimes available. It is more
delicate than _M. argenteus_.

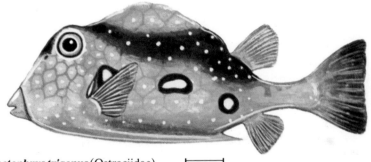

Lactophrys trigonus (Ostraciidae)
Common name: Common trunkfish
Origin: Florida, Caribbean
Size: 30cm (12in)
Community tank: Yes, with
slow-moving species
Food: _Artemia, Mysis_, chopped
foods, some dried food
SG: 1.022–1.025
Invertebrate compatibility: Yes, but
may nip those with feathery
appendages

This species is very common around
the Florida coast and it has long been
popular with American aquarists. Its
peculiar swimming action (see page
36) and well-developed character
make it well worth a place in the
community tank. A similar species,
L. tricornis, is sometimes available,
which has shorter horns than _L.
cornutus_.

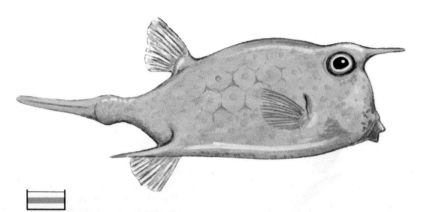

Lactoria cornutus (Ostraciidae)
Common name: Cowfish
Origin: Indo-Pacific Ocean
Size: 45cm (18in)
Community tank: Yes, with
slow-moving species. Will not
compete with greedy eaters
Food: *Artemia, Mysis*, chopped
foods, occasionally takes dried food
SG: 1.020–1.022
Invertebrate compatibility: Yes, but
may nip those with feathery
appendages

This peculiar-looking fish is
justifiably popular. It is easy to keep
provided it is not housed with
boisterous species such as damsels
and larger wrasses. With this species,
as with other Ostraciidae, a clamped
tail fin is normal, and not the sign of
illness it would be among most other
families. Although recorded to 45cm
(18in), cowfish will not normally
outgrow the usual sizes of tank – a
more normal maximum length of
around 15cm (6in) being the norm.
Cowfish invariably become very
tame, and will bob up and down at the
water surface, demanding food.

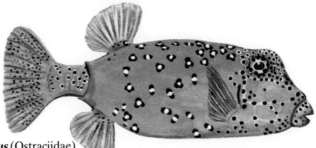

Ostracion cubicus (Ostraciidae)
Common name: Spotted boxfish
Origin: Red Sea, Indo-Pacific Ocean
Size: 45cm (18in)
Community tank: Yes, once properly acclimatised. Keep with slow, placid species
Food: *Artemia, Mysis*, chopped foods, rarely dried food
SG: Red Sea origin 1.025–1.030; otherwise 1.020–1.022
Invertebrate compatibility: Yes, but may nip those with feathery appendages

The illustration shows an adult specimen. It is more commonly available in sizes around 5cm (2in), when the fish shows a bright yellow body, dotted with black spots. *O. cubicus* is instantly appealing, but a word of warning is due. All the *Ostracion* species are capable of exuding a toxic mucus when stressed or dying. If this happens in the community tank then the boxfish and his tank-mates are quickly killed. Having said this, any boxfish which has survived the journey from ocean to pet-shop is unlikely to be unduly stressed by the journey and introduction to the aquarist's tank. Inclusion of this slow swimmer with aggressive species may elicit this poisoning which, in the wild, is merely a defensive reaction towards predators.

Ostracion meleagris (Ostraciidae)
Common name: Orange-spotted boxfish, Black and white boxfish
Origin: Australasia, Indian and Pacific Oceans
Size: 23cm (9in)
Community tank: Yes, with slow-moving, peaceful species
Food: *Artemia, Mysis*, chopped foods, occasionally dried food
SG: 1.020–1.022
Invertebrate compatibility: Yes, but may nip those with feathery appendages

This species is one of the comparative few in which it is easy to tell male from female. The female is a dark blue-black, richly spotted with white. The male is similarly coloured on the back, but has rich yellow-orange spots on a purplish background along the sides. Despite this there have been no reports of successful breeding in aquaria. Like the other Ostraciidae this species gives the impression of a fish locked within an armoured box with only its fins, eyes and mouth protruding.

81

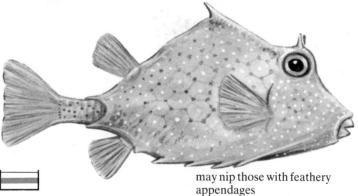

Tetrasomus gibbosus (Ostraciidae)
Common name: Thornback boxfish, Hovercraft
Origin: East Africa, Indo-Pacific Ocean
Size: 30cm (12in) plus
Community tank: Yes, with slow-moving, placid species
Food: Some dried food, otherwise any food small enough to swallow
SG: 1.020–1.022
Invertebrate compatibility: Yes, but

may nip those with feathery appendages

This is probably the hardiest and most easily tamed of the Ostraciidae. It also has the major virtue of being much less inclined to emit toxic mucus than *Ostracion* species. Given a reasonable amount of care *T. gibbosus* is long lived in aquaria and soon learns to take food from its owner's hand. They will blow water at the sand, causing minor sand storms, in the search for food.

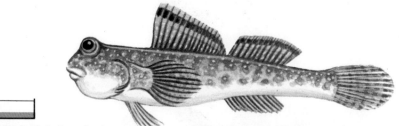

†*Periophthalmus koelreuteri* (Periophthalmidae)
Common name: Mudskipper
Origin: Indo-Pacific Ocean
Size: 13cm (5in)
Community tank: No, requires a specialised habitat
Food: Algae, live worms, insects, insect larvae
SG: 1.010–1.020
Invertebrate compatibility: No; will eat or damage most types

These extremely interesting, occasionally quite colourful, but rare fish are for the more advanced aquarist. In the wild they spend much

of their time out of water, among mangrove roots or on mud banks, where they find much of their food. A similar environment must be provided in captivity, or at the very least there should be a number of places where the fish can leave the water. They will rarely eat anything but live foods and the males, which often have brightly coloured dorsal fins, demand a considerable area as their sole territory. Mudskippers are able to leave the water for considerable lengths of time by virtue of having tightly sealing gill-plates and mouths, which enable their gills to remain damp for long periods.

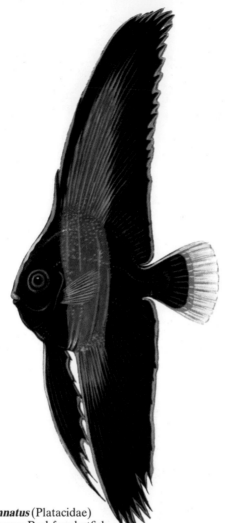

† **Platax pinnatus** (Platacidae)
Common name: Red-face batfish
Origin: Philippines, Indonesia,
Northern Australia
Size: 45cm (18in)
Community tank: No; best kept alone
or with small very peaceful species
which will not damage the delicate
finnage
Food: Almost anything meaty when
settled. Shredded squid is a good first
food
SG: 1.020–1.022
Invertebrate compatibility: Usually
well behaved with most invertebrates
except crustaceans, but some
specimens can be destructive

When small – under 8cm (3in) in
length – *P. pinnatus* must be
included in the top ten most beautiful
marine fish. At this size the body is
velvet black with a vivid scarlet
outline. While the most attractive
member of its family, it is also the
most delicate. Very often it will not
feed properly, but may be tempted by
tiny pieces of squid suspended in
mid-water on the end of a thread.
When properly acclimatised it will
take almost any food, however. A
peaceful, graceful fish.

83

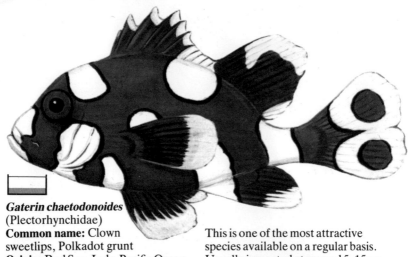

Gaterin chaetodonoides
(Plectorhynchidae)
Common name: Clown
sweetlips, Polkadot grunt
Origin: Red Sea, Indo-Pacific Ocean
Size: 90cm (36in)
Community tank: Yes, with quiet fish
such as *Amphiprion* and *Chaetodon*
species
Food: *Artemia*, chopped shrimps,
chopped shellfish
SG: Red Sea origin 1.025–1.030;
otherwise 1.020–1.022
Invertebrate compatibility: Yes, but
may eat crustaceans when large

This is one of the most attractive
species available on a regular basis.
Usually imported at around 5–15cm
(2–6in) in length, the peculiar
'waddling' swimming action makes it
instantly appealing. Provided it is
feeding well (it extracts food particles
by sifting the gravel), it is a fairly
hardy species, although it demands
good water conditions. Fortunately it
rarely grows more than 30cm (12in)
in captivity, when the colouring
fades.

Gaterin orientalis (Plectorhynchidae)
Common name: Oriental sweetlips,
Spotted sweetlips
Origin: Central Indian and western
Pacific Oceans
Size: 30cm (12in)
Community tank: Yes, with quiet
companions
Food: *Artemia*, chopped shrimps,
shellfish and earthworms
SG: 1.020–1.022
Invertebrate compatibility: Yes, but
large specimens – over 15cm
(6in) – may eat small crustaceans

This, like *P. chaetodonoides*, can be a
difficult fish to acclimatise to
aquarium life but once feeding
satisfactorily they make very
interesting additions to the
community tank. It spends much of
its time swimming gracefully near the
bottom, where it also scavenges,
taking mouthfuls of gravel which it
sifts out through its gills, extracting
any food which other fish may have
missed. When frightened, it rises to
mid-water where it can show a
surprising turn of speed.

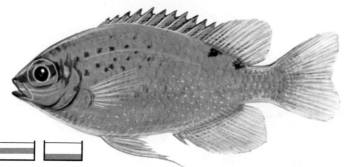

Abudefduf cyanae (Pomacentridae)
Common name: Electric blue damsel, Blue devil
Origin: Indo-Pacific Ocean
Size: 8cm (3in)
Community tank: Yes, one of the best behaved *Abudefduf* species
Food: *Artemia, Mysis*, chopped shellfish, dried food
SG: 1.020–1.022
Invertebrate compatibility: Yes

This is one of the commonest, least expensive and most popular of small marine fish. It is easy to keep, eating almost anything edible, and can be expected to live for several years. The male has a blue tail with a black border and is slimmer than the female (illustrated) which has a clear tail. They spawn quite readily in captivity, the male becoming blotched with dark and light blue colours when displaying to his mate. Eggs are laid inside large shells or inside caves and the fry, although small, have been successfully reared. (See *Amphiprion ocellaris* for breeding hints.) A well-kept pair will spawn at monthly intervals.

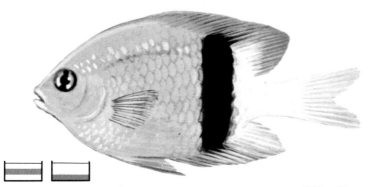

†**Abudefduf dickii** (Pomacentridae)
Common name: Black-bar damsel, Black-bar devil
Origin: Indian and Indo-Pacific Oceans
Size: 13cm (5in)
Community tank: No, becomes very aggressive but can be kept with lively species when small
Food: *Artemia*, chopped shrimp, chopped shellfish, dried food
SG: 1.020–1.022
Invertebrate compatibility: Yes, generally well behaved but large specimens may eat small crustaceans

This is one of the most attractive of the *Abudefduf* species, the anterior part of the body being a rich golden yellow when in good condition. Unfortunately, this lively fish becomes increasingly territorial and will harrass and damage other fish which intrude on their territories.

Abudefduf lacrymatus
(Pomacentridae)
Common name: White-spotted
damsel, Jewelled damsel
Origin: Red Sea, Indian and
Indo-Pacific Oceans
Size: 8cm (3in)
Community tank: Yes, when
small – under 4cm (1½in) – but
somewhat aggressive when adult
Food: *Artemia, Mysis*, chopped
shellfish, dried food
SG: Red Sea origin 1.025–1.030;
otherwise 1.020–1.022

Invertebrate compatibility: Yes,
generally well behaved but large
specimens may eat small crustaceans

Although common throughout its
range this species is rarely imported
as its colours cannot compete with
many other damselfish. They are very
easy fish for the beginner to maintain
successfully. *A. lacrymatus* is often
found in rock pools where it must be
able to adapt to extremes of
temperature and considerable
variation in specific gravity.

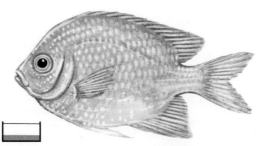

†**Abudefduf leucogaster**
(Pomacentridae)
Common name: Yellow-bellied
damsel, Yellow-bellied devil
Origin: Indo-Pacific Ocean and
Australasia
Size: 15cm (6in)
Community tank: No; inclined to be
scrappy when mature. Small
specimens are only safe with larger
fish
Food: *Mysis*, chopped shrimp,
chopped shellfish, dried food
SG: 1.020–1.022

Invertebrate compatibility: Yes,
generally well behaved but large
specimens may eat small crustaceans

This infrequently imported but hardy
species has never achieved any
degree of popularity, due largely to
its aggressive nature. It vigorously
defends quite extensive territories
and will severely damage persistent
intruders. The colour intensities may
vary from those shown in the
illustration.

Abudefduf oxyodon (Pomacentridae)
Common name: Black neon damsel
Origin: Indo-Pacific Ocean
Size: 15cm (6in)
Community tank: Yes, with similar-sized, lively species
Food: *Artemia, Mysis*, chopped shellfish, dried food
SG: 1.020–1.022
Invertebrate compatibility: Yes, but very large specimens – over 10cm (4in) – may damage small crustaceans

This beautiful fish is one of the most popular damselfish despite regularly outgrowing small aquaria. Lively and inquisitive, it is at its best when young, the white band disappearing at about 5cm (2in) length and the iridescent streaks fading as the fish reaches maturity. Provided plenty of cover is provided small specimens are usually peaceful but they seem to feel insecure in sparsely decorated aquaria and respond aggressively.

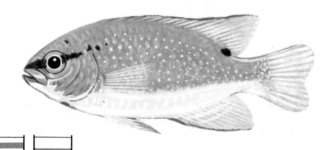

Abudefduf sapphirus
(Pomacentridae)
Common name: Sapphire damsel, Sapphire devil
Origin: Indo-Pacific Ocean
Size: 8cm (3in)
Community tank: Yes, with similar-sized or larger species
Food: *Artemia*, chopped shrimp, chopped shellfish, dried food
SG: 1.020–1.022
Invertebrate compatibility: Yes, generally very well behaved

As a general rule the various blue damselfish tend to be more peaceful than those of other colours and the infrequently seen sapphire damsel is no exception. Rather boisterous when mature it makes an ideal aquarium specimen when young. The intensity and extent of yellow in the belly is quite variable.

†*Abudefduf saxatillis*
(Pomacentridae)
Common name: Sergeant major
Origin: All tropical waters
Size: 17cm (7in)
Community tank: No, except when
very small – under 4cm (1½in)
Food: *Artemia*, chopped shrimp,
chopped shellfish, dried food
SG: 1.020–1.022
Invertebrate compatibility: Yes,
when small but large specimens can
be aggressive – particularly towards
their own species

In the aquarium the sergeant major is
extremely hardy but unfortunately it
grows very large quickly, and then
demands an extensive territory which
it defends from its own and other
species. Sergeant majors have
spawned many times in captivity.
Patches of wine-coloured eggs, about
8cm (3in) in diameter, are guarded by
the male which becomes a deep
blue-black when sexually mature.

†*Abudefduf xanthurus*
(Pomacentridae)
Common name: Orange-tail damsel,
Orange-tail devil
Origin: Indo-Pacific Ocean
Size: 15cm (6in)
Community tank: No, except when
very small – under 4cm (1½in)
Food: *Artemia*, chopped shrimp,
chopped shellfish, dried food
SG: 1.020–1.022
Invertebrate compatibility: Yes,
when small but large specimens can

be aggressive – particularly towards
their own species

This is one of many *Abudefduf*
species which looks quite attractive
when young but loses its appeal as it
grows. When young it has a rich
orange tail and anal area, but with
age this darkens until the fish is
largely brown. *A. xanthurus* is very
hardy but is often aggressive and very
territorial, defending large areas
against all comers.

Amblyglyphidodon aureus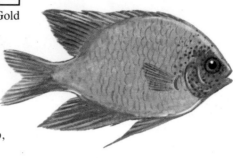
(Pomacentridae)
Common name: Gold damsel, Gold devil
Origin: Indo-Pacific Ocean
Size: 8cm (3in)
Community tank: Yes, when small – 2.5cm (1in) – but large specimens can be aggressive, particularly towards their own species
Food: *Artemia*, chopped shrimp, chopped shellfish, dried food
SG: 1.020–1.022
Invertebrate compatibility: Yes, generally well behaved but large specimens may eat small crustaceans

The two common names reflect the change in behaviour demonstrated by many of the Pomacentridae. American hobbyists tend to call them devils – a fair reflection of their somewhat vicious behaviour as adults. British hobbyists call the group damselfish for when young they are pretty, lively and quite appealing. *A. aureus* is at its best when young; the golden body colour turning a dull green-brown with age.

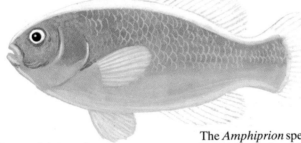

Amphiprion akallopisos
(Pomacentridae)
Common name: Orange skunk clown
Origin: Indo-Pacific Ocean
Size: 8cm (3in)
Community tank: Yes, with similar-sized or smaller peaceful species
Food: Algae, *Artemia, Mysis*, chopped shellfish, dried food
SG: 1.020–1.022
Invertebrate compatibility: Yes, all the *Amphiprion* species are well behaved, but occasional large specimens will eat small crustaceans

The *Amphiprion* species are well known for their symbiotic relationship with sea-anemones, the fish living among the tentacles of these invertebrates which would sting to death and eat other small fish. This particular species is particularly dependent on having a host anemone and rarely prospers if kept without one. Less commonly imported than other *Amphiprion* species, *A. akallopisos* is easily confused with *A. sandaracinos*. They may be distinguished by the white stripe down the dorsal surface; that in *A. akallopisos* tapering out between the eyes, while in *A. sandaracinos* the stripe continues onto the top lip.

Amphiprion chrysopterus
(Pomacentridae)
Common name: Orange-fin clown,
Pacific clown
Origin: South and central Pacific
Ocean
Size: 15cm (6in)
Community tank: Yes, with
similar-sized fish prepared to
compete for food
Food: Algae, *Artemia*, chopped
shrimp, chopped shellfish, dried food
SG: 1.020–1.022
Invertebrate compatibility: Yes, but
may eat small crustaceans

This is one of the largest clownfish. In
the wild it tends to associate with
Condylactis anemones, but in
captivity it settles into the more
commonly available *Radianthus* and
Stoicactis species. Like most of its
genus the pacific clown should be
kept either singly, in compatible
male/female pairs, or in groups of five
or six. Inadvertently housing two of
the same sex together may result in
fierce fighting. A long-lived species.

Amphiprion clarkii (Pomacentridae)
Common name: Chocolate clown,
Yellowtail clown
Origin: Indian, Indo-Pacific and
western Pacific Oceans
Size: 15cm (6in)
Community tank: Yes, with
similar-sized species
Food: Algae, *Artemia, Mysis*,
chopped shellfish, dried food
SG: 1.020–1.022
Invertebrate compatibility: Yes, but
may eat small crustaceans

Chocolate clownfish are hardy fish,
and an ideal species for the newcomer
to marine fishkeeping. The
illustration shows a young specimen.
As *A. clarkii* nears maturity the rich
brown body colour darkens, almost
to black, and the central white band
becomes narrower. Like many of the
Amphiprion species this one has
frequently spawned in captivity and
some fry have been raised. General
conditions for breeding are described
on page 92 under *A. ocellaris*.

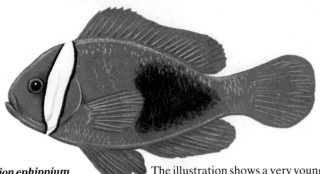

Amphiprion ephippium
(Pomacentridae)
Common name: Tomato clown
Origin: Indo-Pacific Ocean
Size: 15cm (6in)
Community tank: Yes, and will compete with more aggressive fish if these are not disproportionately large
Food: Algae, *Artemia*, chopped shrimp, chopped shellfish, dried food
SG: 1.020–1.022
Invertebrate compatibility: Yes, but large specimens will eat small crustaceans, particularly after shedding their hard exoskeleton

The illustration shows a very young specimen. The white head band fades at about three months, and the dark area in the back spreads until much of the body is dark brown. One of the most aggressive of its genus, it is best kept alone unless a compatible pair is available. Tomato clowns are usually found with *Stoicactis* anemones in the wild but will accept others and, like other larger species, can be successfully maintained without a host anemone. If a pair is housed in a large tank with suitable anemones they will often spawn.

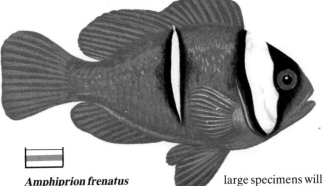

Amphiprion frenatus
(Pomacentridae)
Common name: Fire clown,
Red clown
Origin: Indo-Pacific and western Pacific Oceans
Size: 10cm (4in)
Community tank: Yes, not aggressive but prepared to compete with larger fish
Food: Algae, *Artemia, Mysis*, chopped shellfish, dried food
SG: 1.020–1.022
Invertebrate compatibility: Yes, but large specimens will eat small crustaceans, particularly when they are soft

The illustration shows a young specimen. The centre stripe is rarely maintained after the fish is about 2.5cm (1in) long, but the head stripe is always present. Fire clownfish are one of the hardiest of clowns, and ideal for beginners. Less dependent on anemones than most, they will accept *Radianthus* or *Stoicactis* species.

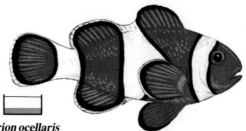

Amphiprion ocellaris
(Pomacentridae)
Common name: Common clown,
Anemonefish
Origin: Indo-Pacific Ocean
Size: 10cm (4in)
Community tank: Yes, an ideal
species and very suitable for
beginners
Food: Algae, *Artemia, Mysis*,
chopped shellfish, dried food
SG: 1.020–1.022
Invertebrate compatibility: Yes,
almost invariably well behaved

This is probably the most popular
species within the marine hobby.
Inexpensive, hardy and
non-aggressive, it is frequently

spawned in captivity. As in all
Amphiprion species, a pair require a
tank of 135l (30 gals) or larger with a
Stoicactis or *Radianthus* anemone
sited near smooth rocks or shells. The
pair will clean the rock, close to the
foot of the anemone, and lay and
fertilise the eggs. The eggs are then
fanned and guarded. Hatching occurs
about nine days later, during the
early hours of the morning. Remove
fry to a small tank where a continual
supply of small live food is available.
Euplotes is usually used. After about
five days the fry will eat *Artemia*
nauplii. After two weeks very finely
shredded frozen foods and powdered
dried foods may be taken.

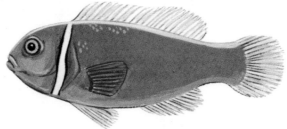

Amphiprion perideraion
(Pomacentridae)
Common name: Pink skunk clown
Origin: Indo-Pacific Ocean
Size: 8cm (3in)
Community tank: Yes, with small,
peaceful species
Food: Algae, *Artemia, Mysis*,
chopped shellfish, dried food
SG: 1.020–1.022
Invertebrate compatibility: Yes,
almost invariably very well behaved
towards all invertebrates

The pink skunk clownfish is one of
very few species which can be
definitively sexed by colour alone.
Mature males show a fine orange rim
around the tail which is absent in the
females. This species must be kept
with an anemone if it is to fare well,
and if a well-kept pair is maintained
they can be expected to spawn quite
regularly. This is probably the most
delicate *Amphiprion* species,
demanding very good water
conditions.

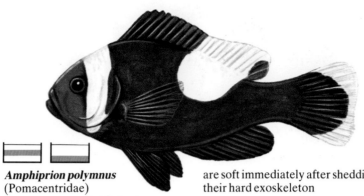

Amphiprion polymnus
(Pomacentridae)
Common name: Saddleback
clownfish
Origin: Indo-Pacific Ocean
Size: 15cm (6in)
Community tank: Yes, with
similar-sized fish
Food: Algae, *Artemia*, chopped
shrimp, chopped shellfish, dried food
SG: 1.020–1.022
Invertebrate compatibility: Yes, but
large specimens will eat small
crustaceans, particularly when they
are soft immediately after shedding
their hard exoskeleton

A. polymnus has not achieved the
popularity of many other
Amphiprion species. Large
specimens are often available,
however, and make good display fish
in large mixed fish and invertebrate
aquaria. Males will often show a good
deal of dull orange around the face
and belly. Of all the larger species this
one is the most dependent upon
having a host anemone.

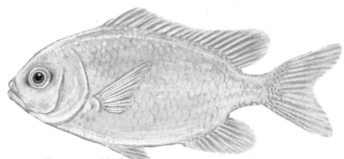

Chromis caeruleus (Pomacentridae)
Common name: Green chromis
Origin: Red Sea, Indian and Pacific
Oceans
Size: 10cm (4in)
Community tank: Yes, but best with
peaceful species
Food: *Artemia*, zooplankton, finely
chopped shrimp, dried food
SG: Red Sea origin 1.025–1.030;
otherwise 1.020–1.022
Invertebrate compatibility: Yes, an
ideal fish for the mixed fish and
invertebrate community

Green chromis form enormous
schools in the wild and fare best in
captivity when kept in groups of six or
more. They like strongly aerated
water and tend to keep to the top
layers of the tank where they take
small particles of food that drift in the
currents. Green is a somewhat
unusual colour among marine fish,
and green chromis fills the demand
for this colour admirably.

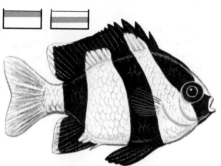

Dascyllus aruanus (Pomacentridae)
Common name: Humbug damsel,
White-tail damsel
Origin: Red Sea, Indian and Pacific
Oceans
Size: 8cm (3in)
Community tank: Yes, when
small – under 4cm (1½in) – but
sometimes aggressive when adult
Food: *Artemia*, chopped shrimp,
chopped shellfish, dried food
SG: Red Sea origin 1.025–1.030;
otherwise 1.020–1.022
Invertebrate compatibility: Yes, very
well behaved when young, but large
specimens will eat small crustaceans
while these are soft immediately after
shedding their hard exoskeleton

Many of the damselfish are seen at
their best when kept in small groups,

and this species is no exception. One
alone is insignificant, but a group of
six or seven youngsters swimming in
and out of corals and emulating
Amphiprion species in an anemone
can be very striking. Unfortunately,
humbugs become increasingly
territorial with age and large
specimens will harass many fish of a
similar size.

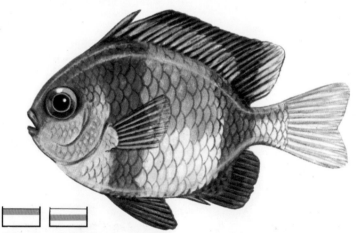

Dascyllus carneus (Pomacentridae)
Common name: Dusky damsel,
White-tail damsel
Origin: Western Indian Ocean
Size: 8cm (3in)
Community tank: Yes, when
small – under 4cm (1½in) – but
sometimes aggressive when adult
Food: *Artemia*, chopped shrimp,
chopped shellfish, dried food
SG: 1.020–1.022
Invertebrate compatibility: Yes, but
large specimens will eat small

crustaceans while these are soft
immediately after shedding their
exoskeleton

When in good condition this is a very
attractive little fish with a violet sheen
over the body. A group of small
specimens in a large tank makes an
attractive collection, but large
specimens are best kept singly.
Dusky damsels are ideal for
beginners, taking a lot of abuse and
being extremely hardy.

Dascyllus melanurus
(Pomacentridae)

Common name: Black-tail humbug damsel
Origin: Indo-Pacific Ocean
Size: 8cm (3in)
Community tank: Yes, when small – under 4cm (1½in) – but only with large boisterous species when adult
Food: _Artemia_, chopped shrimp, chopped fish, dried food
SG: 1.020–1.022
Invertebrate compatibility: Yes, but large specimens will eat small crustaceans while they are soft just after shedding their exoskeleton

Less common than _D. aruanus_ with which it can be confused. _D. melanurus_ is distinguished by its black tail. Apart from this the fish can be considered identical in behaviour, requirements and ease of maintenance. All the common species of _Dascyllus_ have been spawned in captivity, but they cannot easily be sexed. A group of six or seven should be reared together to eventually produce a compatible pair.

Dascyllus trimaculatus
(Pomacentridae)
Common name: Domino damsel
Origin: Red Sea, Indian and Indo-Pacific Oceans
Size: 15cm (6in)
Community tank: Yes, when very small – under 4cm (1½in) – but increasingly territorial as it grows
Food: _Artemia_, chopped shrimp, chopped shellfish, dried food
SG: Red Sea origin 1.025–1.030; otherwise 1.020–1.022
Invertebrate compatibility: Yes, but like other _Dascyllus_ species, large specimens may eat small crustaceans

Domino damsels are very appealing when small but lose their attraction as they grow, many specimens becoming extremely aggressive. When small they will swim among sea-anemones, like _Amphiprion_ species, and the adults often lay their eggs at the base of anemones. The white spots, from which the common name is derived, shrink and disappear with age.

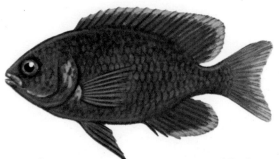

Eupomacentrus fuscus
(Pomacentridae)
Common name: Dusky damsel
Origin: Western Atlantic, Caribbean
Size: 15cm (6in)
Community tank: Yes, when small – under 4cm (1½in) – but aggressive when mature
Food: *Artemia*, chopped shellfish, dried food
SG: 1.022–1.025
Invertebrate compatibility: Yes, but large specimens will eat small crustaceans while they are soft just after shedding their exoskeleton

E. fuscus is very common around the southern United States and often occurs in aquaria there, but it is rarely seen in Europe since it can be quite expensive. Fairly dull when compared with many members of the Pomacentridae, it has the advantage of being extremely hardy although it becomes increasingly aggressive with age.

Eupomacentrus leucostictus
(Pomacentridae)
Common name: Beau Gregory
Origin: Western tropical Atlantic Ocean
Size: 10cm (4in)
Community tank: Yes, with similar-sized, competitive species
Food: *Artemia*, chopped shrimp, chopped shellfish, dried food
SG: 1.020–1.024
Invertebrate compatibility: Yes, but large specimens will eat small crustaceans while they are soft just after shedding their exoskeleton

This is one of the most attractive Atlantic pomacentrids and is one of very few which are regularly imported to Europe. It is a very suitable fish for beginners and a group of six or more small specimens in a well-stocked invertebrate tank makes a very attractive collection. It is a very eager feeder and care must be taken that more placid species get a fair share of the available food.

Microspathodon chrysurus
(Pomacentridae)
Common name: Jewelfish, Atlantic yellow-tail damsel
Origin: Caribbean
Size: 17cm (7in)
Community tank: Yes when small – under 8cm (3in) – but becomes increasingly aggressive with age
Food: *Artemia*, chopped shrimp, chopped shellfish, dried food
SG: 1.022–1.025
Invertebrate compatibility: Yes, but large specimens may eat small crustaceans

Jewelfish are very popular among American hobbyists but less so in Europe where they are among the most expensive pomacentrids. They are very pretty little fish when young, with iridescent light blue spots on a dark blue body. When mature the fish is brown with a bright yellow tail. At any size jewelfish will not tolerate the presence of their own kind.

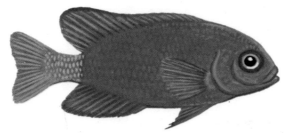

Pomacentrus melanochir
(Pomacentridae)
Common name: Yellow-tail damsel
Origin: Indian Ocean
Size: 10cm (4in)
Community tank: Yes, with equally competitive species
Food: *Artemia, Mysis*, chopped shellfish, dried food
SG: 1.020–1.022
Invertebrate compatibility: Yes, safe with most invertebrates regardless of the fish's size

They are an attractive purple-blue when young, but a brown cast develops over the body as they age. Cheap and hardy, they are, however, one of the less placid blue damselfish and should only be kept with species which are able to compete successfully for food and territories. This species may be confused with the common Philippines yellow-tail damsel but the latter is brighter blue, shorter in the body and much more peaceful.

Pomacentrus pavo (Pomacentridae)
Common name: Pavo damsel
Origin: Australasia, Indo-Pacific
Ocean
Size: 13cm (5in)
Community tank: Yes, with
similar-sized, lively species
Food: *Artemia*, chopped shrimp,
chopped shellfish, dried food
SG: 1.020–1.022
Invertebrate compatibility: Yes,
generally well behaved but will eat
small crustaceans

This species is very variable in its
colouring and is more commonly seen
in a bluer form than in the
illustration, the body being a rich
cobalt blue with yellow around the
tail and belly. Although a good
aquarium fish it is not imported
regularly and commands a
comparatively high price.

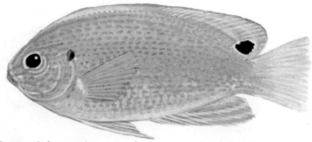

Pomacentrus vaiuli (Pomacentridae)
Common name: Ocellate damsel
Origin: Indo-Pacific and western
Pacific Oceans
Size: 10cm (4in)
Community tank: Yes, with lively
species
Food: *Artemia, Mysis*, chopped
shellfish, dried food
SG: 1.020–1.022
Invertebrate compatibility: Yes,
generally very well behaved

Only scarcity of supplies prevents *P.
vaiuli* from becoming one of the most
popular damselfish. It is beautifully
coloured and less aggressive than
many species, but is rarely imported
to Europe because its natural range
does not fall within the major
collecting areas. Like most of the
pomacentrids the ocellate damsel
should be kept either singly or in
groups of six or more of the same
species. Different species can
normally be mixed quite
satisfactorily.

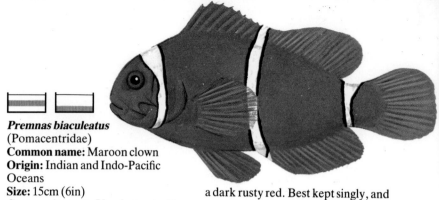

Premnas biaculeatus
(Pomacentridae)
Common name: Maroon clown
Origin: Indian and Indo-Pacific Oceans
Size: 15cm (6in)
Community tank: Yes, but not with other clownfish
Food: Algae, *Artemia*, chopped shrimp, chopped shellfish, dried food
SG: 1.020–1.022
Invertebrate compatibility: Yes, but large specimens will eat small crustaceans

When young this is an extremely attractive species, being a rich, intense red, but this often changes to a dark rusty red. Best kept singly, and away from other clownfish, since it is often extremely aggressive to others of its kind. The maroon clown will often refuse to settle into the commonly available *Radianthus* species but will usually move into *Stoicactis* species quite readily. It is much less dependant on anemones for its well-being than many of its relations. Clownfish have a mucus which seems to inhibit the firing of the anemone's stinging cells.

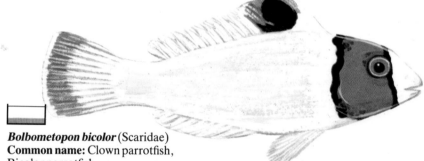

Bolbometopon bicolor (Scaridae)
Common name: Clown parrotfish, Bicolor parrotfish
Origin: Red Sea, Indo-Pacific Ocean
Size: 60cm (24in)
Community tank: Yes, but occasional large specimens may nip tank-mates
Food: Algae, chopped shrimps, chopped shellfish, earthworms
SG: Red Sea origin 1.025–1.030; otherwise 1.020–1.022
Invertebrate compatibility: Only the very smallest specimens, under 5cm (2in), should be considered for the invertebrate tank and even then they should not be housed with live corals.

This attractive fish is at its best when young. Specimens around 15cm (6in) long become greyish-yellow, instead of white, and the scarlet head band turns more towards rust brown. The adult male is green with flesh-pink spots and stripes. It is easy to feed, and its constant nibbling at the rocks will tend to prevent excessive algal growth. Vegetable matter is an important part of the diet and must be provided if there is little algae present.

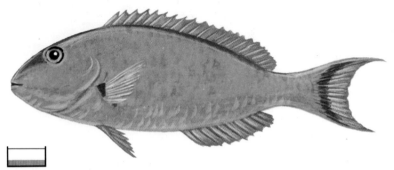

Sparisoma chrysopterum (Scaridae)
Common name: Redtail parrotfish
Origin: Tropical western·Atlantic
Size: 45cm (18in)
Community tank: Yes, but some
individuals are belligerent
Food: Algae, shrimps, shellfish
SG: 1.022–1.025
Invertebrate compatibility: Not
compatible

The illustration shows an adult male.
The female and young males are
much duller so this species only
appeals to aquarists with very large
tanks. The hard, parrotbeak-like
jaws are developed to feed on live
corals, and parrotfish are generally
considered major causes of natural
reef erosion.

Sparisoma viride (Scaridae)
Common name: Stoplight parrotfish
Origin: Tropical western Atlantic
Size: 50cm (20in)
Community tank: Yes, but some
individuals are belligerent
Food: Algae, shrimps, shellfish
SG: 1.022–1.025
Invertebrate compatibility: Not
compatible

This beautiful species is very common
in the West Indies and is regularly

available to American hobbyists. It is
less often seen in Europe. The
illustration shows an adult male, but
the common name is derived from the
colours of the female. She has a
bright red belly contrasting with a
dull brownish back. The natural diet
of all *Sparisoma* species is living coral
and some specimens are reluctant to
take alternative foods, although most
will learn to take the commercially
available fare.

Scatophagus argus (Scatophagidae)
Common name: Spotted scat
Origin: Indian and Indo-Pacific
Oceans
Size: 25cm (10in)
Community tank: Yes, with
other lively species
Food: Almost any normal fish food
SG: 1.005–1.022
Invertebrate compatibility: Yes,
when small, but most specimens will
damage finely structured
invertebrates, and larger ones will eat
small crustaceans

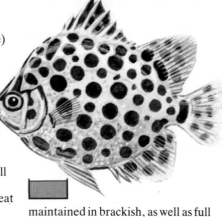

This is one of the hardiest and
cheapest marine fish available. It is
peaceful and easy to feed, an
indication of this being found in the
specific name which translated
literally means 'hundred-eyed
muck-eater'. It can be successfully
maintained in brackish, as well as full
strength, sea-water. A variety known
as the red or tiger scat is sometimes
available, which shows varying
degrees of rust-red markings in the
fins and around the dark spots. These
are particularly attractive when
small. It will quickly devour
decorative algae.

Equetus lanceolatus (Sciaenidae)
Common name: Ribbonfish,
Jack-knifefish
Origin: Caribbean, tropical western
Atlantic Ocean
Size: 25cm (10in)
Community tank: Yes, with
similar-sized, peaceful species
Food: *Artemia*, chopped shrimp,
chopped shellfish, occasionally dried
food
SG: 1.020–1.025
Invertebrate compatibility: No,
may damage invertebrates
other than coelenterates

Less common and somewhat more
delicate than many of its relations,
the ribbonfish is still a very desirable
species. It is a little shy and will not
compete with more aggressive
species for food, but a group of five or
six makes a very elegant collection.
The dorsal fin is proportionately
longest when the fish is young. Young
specimens can sometimes be difficult
to acclimatise but will usually accept
live *Artemia*. A somewhat smaller
and more common species, *E.
acuminatus*, the high hat, has
spawned in captivity but no fry were
reared. The parents rapidly circle
each other until they come into
contact when, with jaws quivering,
the eggs, which sink to the substrate,
are released.

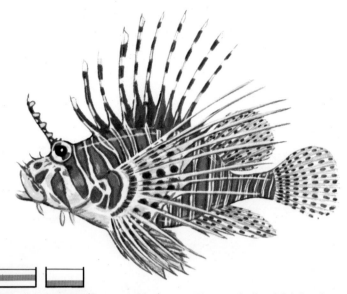

Pterois antennata (Scorpaenidae)
Common name: Spotfin lionfish
Origin: Indian and western Pacific Oceans
Size: 20.5cm (8in)
Community tank: Yes, with fish large enough not to be swallowed, and which would not nip at *P. antennata*'s extended finnage
Food: Fish, shrimps
SG: 1.020–1.022
Invertebrate compatibility: Yes, but will eat crustaceans

The spotfin lionfish is less frequently imported than the following species and it is also somewhat more difficult to feed; this species is often reluctant to take dead food. Once established, *P. antennata* should prove a long-lived and spectacular addition to the tank. Great care should be taken when servicing the lionfish tank to avoid punctures from the venomous dorsal spines.

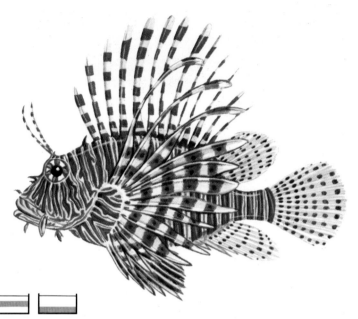

Pterois volitans (Scorpaenidae)
Common name: Peacock lionfish, Turkeyfish, Scorpionfish, Butterfly cod
Origin: Red Sea, Indian and Pacific Oceans
Size: 38cm (15in)
Community tank: Yes, with species large enough not to be swallowed
Food: Fish, shrimps
SG: Red Sea origin 1.025–1.030; otherwise 1.020–1.022
Invertebrate compatibility: Yes, but will eat crustaceans

P. volitans is justifiably one of the most popular marine fish. Its spectacular colouring, finnage and awesome reputation as being dangerously venomous ensures that it is always the centre of attention. All *Pterois* species are nocturnal or crepuscular, leaving caves and crevices at dawn and dusk to feed on small fish and shrimps. This species soon learns to take dead food as it falls through the water. Some specimens will even take dried foods. All of the *Pterois* species dislike strong light and may go blind if over-illuminated for too long.

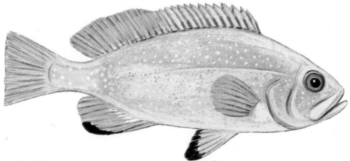

Calloplesiops altivelus (Serranidae)
Common name: Comet grouper,
Celestial grouper, Saltwater betta
Origin: Indo-Pacific Ocean
Size: 30cm (12in)
Community tank: Yes, but not with
very small species, as these may be
eaten
Food: Fish, shrimps, earthworms
SG: 1.020–1.022
Invertebrate compatibility: Yes,
except with crustaceans which may
well be eaten

This beautiful, but unfortunately
rare, species is one of the few
groupers which can safely be
considered for the community tank.
Often initially shy, it eventually
tames, but a shaded hiding place
should be provided. When stalking
food *C. altivelus* shows why it is
sometimes called the saltwater betta.
It spreads its fins to their fullest and
curves the body into a semicircle
while slowly advancing on its prey. In
this posture *C. altivelus* is one of the
most visually striking of marine fish.

†*Epinephelus flavocaeruleus*
(Serranidae)
Common name: Powder blue
grouper, Blue and yellow reef-cod
Origin: Indo-Pacific Ocean
Size: 45cm (18in)
Community tank: No
Food: Fish, shrimps, whole shellfish
SG: 1.020–1.022
Invertebrate compatibility: Yes, but
will eat crustaceans

E. flavocaeruleus is less frequently
available than many Serranidae and it
commands a comparatively high
price. This species displays typical
grouper behaviour in that it will rest,
almost motionless, among rocks for
long periods then rush out and engulf
its food. Powder-blue groupers are
often shy when first introduced to the
tank but usually become tame
enough to take hand-held food. *E.
flavocaeruleus* is by far the most
attractive member of its genus.

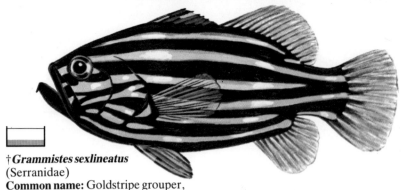

† *Grammistes sexlineatus*
(Serranidae)
Common name: Goldstripe grouper,
Sixline grouper
Origin: Indo-Pacific Ocean
Size: 30cm (12in)
Community tank: No. Will eat or
harass more peaceful species
Food: Fish, shrimps, shellfish
SG: 1.020–1.022
Invertebrate compatibility: Yes, but
will eat crustaceans

This is one of the most commonly
imported groupers but is often shy,
hiding under rocks for much of the
day. It has a large mouth and can
swallow a fish at least half its own
size. When stressed, the goldstripe
grouper can produce large quantities
of toxic mucus, and tank-mates may
be poisoned by it.

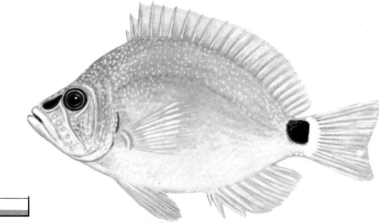

Hypoplectrus unicolor (Serranidae)
Common name: Butter hamlet
Origin: Caribbean
Size: 15cm (6in)
Community tank: Yes, with
similar-sized, lively and competitive
species. Should not be kept with
small fish which may be eaten
Food: Fish, shrimps
SG: 1.022–1.025
Invertebrate compatibility: Yes, but
will eat crustaceans

The butter hamlet is the commonest,

but least colourful, of an interesting
genus which extends throughout
Florida and the West Indies. Their
main claim to fame is that they are
functional hermaphrodites. They
normally spawn, two together, in the
wild, but theoretically they can
fertilise their own eggs so there is the
possibility of one isolated captive
hamlet producing fry. More
attractive members of the genus are
H. chlorurus (yellowtail hamlet), and
H. gummigutta (golden hamlet).

†*Serranus scriba* (Serranidae)
Common name: Comber
Origin: Tropical Atlantic and Mediterranean
Size: 45cm (18in)
Community tank: No, this is a voracious and efficient predator
Food: Fish, shrimps
SG: 1.020–1.025
Invertebrate compatibility: Yes, but will eat crustaceans

S. scriba is only rarely available to the hobbyist but it is occasionally seen in public aquaria where it makes a long-lived if somewhat lethargic exhibit. *S. scriba* is never expensive and is extremely hardy, so it may appeal to the beginner looking for a large character fish.

---

†*Hippocampus kuda* (Syngnathidae)
Common name: Common seahorse, Oceanic seahorse
Origin: Indian and Pacific Oceans as far north as Japan
Size: 13cm (5in); locally 30cm (12in)
Community tank: No, may only be kept with very quiet, non-competitive species such as small blennies, gobies and *Amphiprion* species
Food: *Artemia, Mysis*
SG: 1.020–1.022
Invertebrate compatibility: Yes, but large crustaceans may eat them

Seahorses are among the most intriguing fish available to the hobbyist. Visually totally dissimilar to other fish, they are unique in that it is the male which gives birth to the young. The female places fertilised eggs in a pouch on the male's belly. Here the eggs develop, until miniature replicas of the parents are expelled. This has often been witnessed in the home aquarium and the young have occasionally been raised. *Euplotes* should be used as food for the first week, followed by copious feedings with newly hatched *Artemia* nauplii. Although baby seahorses will engulf the nauplii at birth they cannot digest them at this stage.

† **Hippocampus zosterae**
(Syngnathidae)
Common name: Dwarf seahorse
Origin: Western Atlantic, Caribbean
Size: 4cm (1½in)
Community tank: No, best kept with their own kind only
Food: *Artemia*
SG: 1.022–1.025
Invertebrate compatibility: Yes, but avoid crustaceans which may eat them

The dwarf seahorse is very popular in the United States where it is inexpensive, easily obtained and can be successfully maintained in containers which would be considered much too small for any other marine fish. It is less frequently imported to Europe. Providing a regular supply of live *Artemia* can be maintained it is fairly hardy, although short-lived. The fry can be fed with *Artemia* nauplii. In the tank dwarf seahorses will perch on sea-whips and corals, holding on with their prehensile tails.

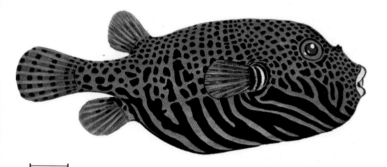

† **Arothron aerostaticus**
(Tetraodontidae)
Origin: Indo-Pacific Ocean
Size: 25cm (10in)
Community tank: No, only with large but non-aggressive species
Food: Shrimp, shellfish, fish, earthworms
SG: 1.020–1.022
Invertebrate compatibility: Will damage and eat most invertebrates except large sea-anemones

All the *Arothron* species are equipped with a set of razor-sharp teeth which, although designed to deal with shrimps and shellfish, can just as easily remove large pieces from unwary fish or fingers. They tame very quickly and soon learn to take food from their owner's hand, but care should still be taken. Swimming appears to be a great effort to all the *Arothron* species and they will often spend much of the time resting on the substrate.

107

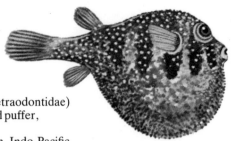

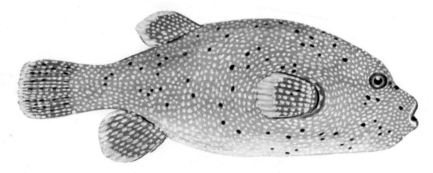

†*Arothron hispidus* (Tetraodontidae)
Common name: Striped puffer,
Fugu-fish
Origin: Red Sea, Indian, Indo-Pacific
and central Pacific Oceans
Size: 38cm (15in)
Community tank: No, only keep with
large, moderately peaceful species
Food: Shrimp, shellfish, fish,
earthworms
SG: Red Sea origin 1.025–1.030;
otherwise 1.020–1.022
Invertebrate compatibility: Will
damage and eat most invertebrates
except large sea-anemones

Despite the internal organs, and
possibly the flesh, being extremely
poisonous, highly trained and
government licensed Japanese chefs
make the much-valued dish Fugu
from this fish. *A. hispidus* becomes
very tame and is very long-lived in
captivity. The illustration shows the
fish distressed and inflated with
water.

†*Arothron nigropunctatus*
(Tetraodontidae)
Common name: Black-spotted puffer
Origin: Indo-Pacific Ocean
Size: 30cm (12in)
Community tank: No, only keep with
large, moderately peaceful species
Food: Shrimp, shellfish, fish,
earthworms
SG: 1.020–1.022
Invertebrate compatibility: Will
damage and eat most invertebrates
except large sea-anemones

When alarmed, this fish inflates its
stomach with water to give the
appearance of a grey-brown flabby
football. This is a fright reaction
which should never be deliberately
evoked. When seeking food
Arothron species will blow a jet of
water at the gravel in an effort to
uncover suitable crustaceans or
molluscs. The sharp, strong teeth are
well-adapted to such fare.

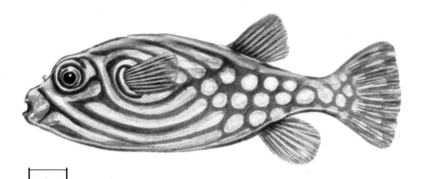

†*Arothron reticulatus*
(Tetraodontidae)
Common name: Reticulated puffer
Origin: Indo-Pacific Ocean
Size: 45cm (18in)
Community tank: No, only keep with large non-aggressive species
Food: Shrimp, shellfish, fish, earthworms
SG: 1.020–1.022
Invertebrate compatibility: Will damage and eat most invertebrates except large sea-anemones

The interesting body pattern makes this one of the most attractive *Arothron* species, particularly as the dark stripes are often a deeper red than shown in the illustration. It tames very quickly, and will eat prodigious amounts of food if allowed to, but may regurgitate the food if over-fed. Tetraodontids are lazy swimmers, normally using only their dorsal and anal fins to cruise slowly around the tank.

Index

Page numbers in italics refer to
    illustrations

Abudefduf cyanae 33, 85, *85*
    dickii 85, *85*
    lacrymatus 86, *86*
    leucogaster 86, *86*
    oxyodon 33, 87, *87*
    sapphirus 87, *87*
    saxatillis 88, *88*
    xanthurus 88, *88*
Acanthuridae 13, 34, 39–42
Acanthurus achilles 39, *39*
    leucosternon 33, 40, *40*
    lineatus 33, 41, *41*
    olivaceus 33, 40, *40*
Acclimatisation 21, 22, *31*
Aeoliscus strigatus 50, *50*
Aeration 12
Air lift 10, 17, 18
    pump 15, 17, 18
Airstone *11*, 12
Algae, 6, 9, 13, 20, 23, 28, 31–3
    fertiliser 18, 23
Amblyglyphidodon aureus 89,
    89
Ammonia 9
    poisoning 8
Amphiprion 26, 27, 29
    akallopisos 33, 89, *89*
    chrysopterus 90, *90*
    clarkii 33, 90, *90*
    ephippium 91, *91*
    frenatus 91, *91*
    ocellaris 32, 92, *92*
    perideraion 92, *92*
    polymnus 93, *93*
Anemone fish 92, *92*
Angel, black 53, *53*, 67, *67*
    black-banded 65, *65*
    blue-girdled 63, *63*
    butterfly 62, *62*
    cherub 51, *51*
    emperor 68, *68*
    fireball 51, *51*
    flagfin 50, *50*
    flame-back 51, *51*
    French 69, *69*
    grey 67, *67*
    koran 69, *69*
    lemonpeel 52, *52*, 53, *53*
    majestic 63, *63*
    Malayan 79, *79*
    orange-tail 62, *62*
    pygmy 51, *51*

regal 70, *70*
    royal empress 70, *70*
    three-spot 50, *50*
    Tibicen 53, *53*
    yellow-tail 62, *62*
Angelfish, dusky 52, *52*
    golden 53, *53*
Apogon fasciatus 42, *42*
Apogonidae 34, 42, 43
Apolemichthys trimaculatus 50,
    50
Aquarium 5, 6, 13, 17, 18
    hood 6, *14*
    salt 7
    siting 6
    stand 5
Arothron 38
    aerostaticus 107, *107*
    hispidus 108, *108*
    nigropunctatus 108, *108*
    reticulatus 109, *109*

Bacteria 12, 18, 24 *see also*
    Infection
Balistapus undulatus 43, *43*
Balistes vetula 44, *44*
Balistidae 34, 43–7
Balistoides niger 44, *44*
Bannerfish 64, *64*
    humphead 65, *65*
Barred jack 49, *49*
Beau Gregory 96, *96*
Blenniidae 34, 47, 48
Blennius cristatus 47, *47*
    nigriceps 48, *48*
Blenny 21
    cardinal 48, *48*
    carmine 48, *48*
Blue and yellow reef-cod 104,
    104
Bodianus axillaris 33, 73, *73*
    rufus 73, *73*
Bolbometopon bicolor 33, 99,
    99
Boxfish 36
    black and white 81, *81*
    orange-spotted 81, *81*
    spotted 81, *81*
    thornback 82, *82*
Buffer solution 8, 18
Butter hamlet 105, *105*
Butterfly, blackback 56, *56*
    black wedge 56, *56*
    bluestriped 57, *57*
    citron 55, *55*
    copperband 63, *63*

eight-banded 59, *59*
foureye 54, *54*
lemon 55, *55*
lined 57, *57*
marleys 58, *58*
moon 58, *58*
neon-banded 60, *60*
ocellate 66, *66*
one-spot 61, *61*
ornate 60, *60*
Pakistan 55, *55*
rainbow 61, *61*
redfin 61, *61*
red-striped 58, *58*
saddleback 56, *56*
speckled 55, *55*
spotfin 59, *59*
tear-drop 61, *61*
threadfin 54, *54*
vagabond 62, *62*
yellow long-nosed 64, *64*
Butterfly cod 103, *103*
Butterflyfish 35

Calloplesiops altivelus 104, *104*
Cantherines sandwichiensis 78,
    78
Canthigaster solandri 48, *48*
    valentini 33, 49, *49*
Canthigasteridae 35, 48, 49
Carangidae 35, 49
Cardinal, pyjama 43, *43*
    spotted 43, *43*
Centriscidae 35, 50
Centropyge acanthops 33, 51,
    51
    argi 51, *51*
    bispinosus 52, *52*
    flavissimus 32, 52, *52*
    heraldi 33, 53, *53*
    tibicen 53, *53*
Chaetodon auriga 32, 54, *54*
    capistratus 54, *54*
    citrinellus 55, *55*
    collaris 33, 55, *55*
    ephippium 56, *56*
    falcula 56, *56*
    fremblii 57, *57*
    lineolatus 57, *57*
    lunula 58, *58*
    marleyi 58, *58*
    ocellatus 59, *59*
    octofasciatus 59, *59*
    ornatissimus 60, *60*
    quadrimaculatus 60, *60*
    speculum 61, *61*

trifasciatus 61, *61*
vagabundus 33, 62, *62*
Chaetodontidae 13, 35, 50–70
Chaetodontoplus mesoleucus 62, *62*
Charcoal 12, 15, 18
Chelmon rostratus 63, *63*
Chromis caeruleus 93, *93*
Clown, chocolate 90, *90*
  common 92, *92*
  fire 91, *91*
  maroon 99, *99*
  orange-fin 90, *90*
  pacific 90, *90*
  pink skunk 92, *92*
  red 91, *91*
  spine-cheeked 99, *99*
  tomato 91, *91*
  yellowtail 90, *90*
Clownfish 21, 27, 29, 37
  saddleback 93, *93*
Coelenterate 29
Comber 106, *106*
Combination system 12
Combined heater and
  thermostat unit 13 ·
Common trunkfish 79, *79*
Condensation 6
  trap 6, *6*
Coral 19, *19*, 20, 22, 30
  beauty 52, *52*
Coris angulata 33, 74, *74*
  formosa 74, *74*
  gaimard 32, 75, *75*
  julis 75, *75*
Cowfish 36, 80, *80*
Croaker 38
Crustacean 27

Damsel, atlantic yellowtail 97, *97*
  black-bar 85, *85*
  black neon 87, *87*
  black-tail humbug 95, *95*
  domino 95, *95*
  dusky 94, *94*, 96, *96*
  electric blue 85, *85*
  gold 89, *89*
  humbug 94, *94*
  jewelled 86, *86*
  ocellate 98, *98*
  orange-tail 88, *88*
  pavo 98, *98*
  sapphire 87, *87*
  white-spotted 86, *86*
  white-tail 94, *94*
  yellow-bellied 86, *86*
  yellow-tail 97, *97*
Damsel fish 21, 37
Dascyllus aruanus 33, 94, *94*
  carneus 94, *94*
  melanurus 95, *95*
  trimaculatus 95, *95*
Devil, black-bar 85, *85*
  blue 85, *85*
  gold 89, *89*

orange-tail 88, *88*
sapphire 87, *87*
yellow-bellied 86, *86*
Devil fish 37
Diodon histrix 33, 70, *70*
Diodontidae 35, 70
Disease 13, 24–6 *see also*
  Infection

Echinoderm 28
Emperor snapper 77, *77*
Epinephelus flavocaeruleus 104, *104*
Equetus lanceolatus 101, *101*
Eupomacentrus fuscus 96, *96*
  leucostictus 96, *96*
Euxiphipops navarchus 33, 63, *63*
Evaporation 6
Excreta 9

Filefish 36
  common 78, *78*
  longnose 78, *78*
  orange-spotted 78, *78*
Filter, biological 10
  diatom 15
  mechanical 10
  power 10–12, 15, 16
  pump 12
  undergravel 9–11, *11*, 12, 17
  wool 10, 12, 15
Filter-plate 17
Filtration 7, 10
Fish, parts of *22*
Fluke 25
Fluorescent tube 14
Food, 23
Forcipiger flavissimus 64, *64*
Fugu-fish 108, *108*

Gaterin chaetodonoides 32, 84, *84*
  orientalis 84, *84*
Gnathodon speciosus 49, *49*
Gobiidae 35, 71
Gobiosoma oceanops 32, 71, *71*
Goby 21, 35
  Catalina 71, *71*
  neon 71, *71*
Golden caranx 49, *49*
Gomphosus coeruleus 76, *76*
Grammistes sexlineatus 105, *105*
Green chromis 93, *93*
Grouper 15, 26
  celestial 104, *104*
  comet 104, *104*
  goldstripe 105, *105*
  powder blue 104, *104*
  sixline 105, *105*

Heating 13
Heater 13, 15, 18
Hemibalistes chrysopterus 45, *45*

Hemigymnus melapterus 76, *76*
Heniochus acuminatus 64, *64*
  varius 65, *65*
Hippocampus kuda 33, 107, *107*
  zosterae 107, *107*
Hog fish, coral 73, *73*
  Spanish 73, *73*
Holacanthus arcuatus 65, *65*
  tricolor 66, *66*
Holocentridae 36, 72
Holocentrus ascensionis 72, *72*
Hovercraft 82, *82*
Humu-humu 46, *46*
Hydrometer 7, 8, 18
Hypoplectrus unicolor 105, *105*

Infection, bacterial 15, 24, 25
  fungal 15, 24, 25
  parasitic 24
  viral 24, 25
Invertebrate 6, 8, 12–14, 20, 23, 27, 32, 33

Jack-knifefish 101, *101*
Jewelfish 97, *97*

Labridae 36, 73–7
Labroides dimidiatus 33, 77, *77*
Lactophrys trigonus 79, *79*
Lactoria cornutus 32, 80, *80*
Leatherjacket 36
Lighting 13–15, 23
Lionfish 38
  peacock 103, *103*
  spotfin 102, *102*
Lutjanidae 36, 77
Lutjanus sebae 77, *77*
Lythrypnus dalli 33, 71, *71*

Maturation 18
Melichthys vidua 45, *45*
Mercury vapour lamp 14
Microspathodon chrysurus 97, *97*
Mollusc 29
Molly Miller 47, *47*
Monacanthidae 36, 78
Mono 79, *79*
Mondactylidae 36, 79
Monodactylus argenteus 79, *79*
Moonfish 79, *79*
Mudskipper 37, 82, *82*
Myripristis murdjan 72, *72*

Naso brevirostris 41, *41*
  lituratus 42, *42*
Natural system 12
Nitrification 12
Nitrogen cycle 9

Odonus niger 33, 46, *46*
Oodinium 24
Orange skunk clown 89, *89*
Ostraciidae 36, 79–82

Ostracion cubicus 81, *81*
  meleagris 81, *81*
Oxymonacanthus longirostris
  33, 78, *78*
Ozoniser 11, 15

Parachaetodon ocellatus 66, *66*
Parrotfish 37
  bicolor 99, *99*
  clown 99, *99*
  redtail 100, *100*
  stoplight 100, *100*
Periophthalmidae 37, 82
Periophthalmus koelreuteri 82,
  82
pH 7–9, 18, 22, 27, 30
Pipefish 38
Plant 8, 31
Platacidae 37, 83
Platax pinnatus 32, 83, *83*
Plectorhynchidae 37, 84
Polkadot grunt 84, *84*
Pomacanthus arcuatus 67, *67*
  imperator 33, 68, *68*
  paru 69, *69*
  semicirculatus 69, *69*
Pomacentridae 37, 85–99
Pomacentrus melanochir 96, *96*
  pavo 98, *98*
  vaiuli 98, *98*
Pop-eye 26
Premnas biaculeatus 99, *99*
Protein skimmer 11, 12, 15, *16*
Pterois antennata 33, 102, *102*
  volitans 32, 103, *103*
Puffer 35
  black-spotted 108, *108*
  margarita 48, *48*
  porcupine 70, *70*
  reticulated 109, *109*
  sharp-nosed 48, *48*
  striped 108, *108*
  valentine 49, *49*
Pygoplites diacanthus 70, *70*

Red emperor 77, *77*
Red-face batfish 83, *83*
Reverse-flow system 12
Rhineacanthus aculeatus 32, 46,
  46
Ribbonfish 101, *101*

Rock 20
  beauty 66, *66*
  'living' 18, 20

Saltwater betta 104, *104*
Scaridae 37, 99, 100
Scatophagidae 38, 101
Scatophagus argus 101, *101*
Sciaenidae 38, 101
Scorpaenidae 38, 102, 103
Scorpionfish 38, 103, *103*
Seahorse 38
  common 106, *106*
  dwarf 107, *107*
  oceanic 106, *106*
Sea Kite 79, *79*
Sea-salt 18
Sea-water 7, 8
Semi-natural system 12
Sergeant major 88, *88*
Serranidae 38, 104–6
Serranus scriba 106, *106*
Shell 19
Shrimpfish 35
Silicon rubber adhesive 5
Smoothhead unicornfish 42, *42*
Soldierfish 36
Sparisoma chrysopterum 100,
  100
  viride 100, *100*
Specific gravity 8, 9, 18, 21, 22,
  31
Spotted scat 101, *101*
Squirrelfish 36
  bigeye 72, *72*
  longjaw 72, *72*
Stability 9
Steriliser, ultra-violet 15
Stonefish 38
Striped cardinalfish 42, *42*
Sufflamen bursa 47, *47*
Surgeon, clown, 41, *41*
  olive 40, *40*
  powder blue 40, *40*
  red-tailed 39, *39*
Surgeon fish 34
Sweetlips, clown 84, *84*
  oriental 84, *84*
  spotted 84, *84*
Syngnathidae 38, 106, 107

Tang 34
  Achilles 39, *39*
  Japanese 42, *42*
  lipstick 42, *42*
  pyjama 41, *41*
  shoulder 40, *40*
  turkeyfish 103, *103*
  unicorn 41, *41*
Temperature 9, 13, 18, 21
Tetraodontidae 38, 107–9
Tetrasomus gibbosus 82, *82*
Thermometer 13, 18
Thermostat 13, 18
Trace element 7, 8, 18
Trigger, black, 46, *46*
  blue 46, *46*
  bursa 47, *47*
  clown 44, *44*
  gold-finned 45, *45*
  green 46, *46*
  Picasso 46, *46*
  pink-tailed 45, *45*
  queen 44, *44*
  sandwich 78, *78*
  undulate 43, *43*
  white-lined 47, *47*
Triggerfish 15, 26
Trunkfish 36

Ultra-violet steriliser 16

Vitamin supplement 18

Waste product 9, 10, 15, 18
Water 7, 8
  pump 16
  salt 8, 18, 19, 24
  tap 8
White spot 24
Wimplefish 64, *64*
  brown 65, *65*
Worm 30
Wrasse 21
  apartheid 76, *76*
  birdnose 76, *76*
  cleaner 77, *77*
  clown 74, *74*, 75, *75*
  half and half 76, *76*
  mediterranean 75, *75*
  twinspot 74, *74*